The Mind of an Innovator:
A Guide to Seeing Possibilities
Where None Existed Before

Patricia Harmon, Ph.D.

Strategic Book Group

Strategic Book Group
P.O. Box 333
Durham CT 06422
www.StrategicBookClub.com

ISBN: 978-1-60911-184-7

Printed in the United States of America

Book Design: Stacie Tingen

Any resemblance of any of the characters appearing in this novel to
living persons is purely coincidental.

To my mother, whose selfless love and strength always shine through.

Acknowledgements

My gratitude extends to many people who over the years have inspired me to write this book. First among them is Edward de Bono, whose pioneering work in thinking techniques unleashed my own thinking and changed the course of my life. I am also grateful to the faculty at The Fielding Graduate Institute, particularly Steven Schapiro and Barnett Pearce, for urging me to think far beyond what I thought were my limitations during the writing of my dissertation, and introducing me to social constructionism.

A thank you goes to Jeanne Pinder, whose editorial prowess and patience amazed me. To Gregory Thompson, the consummate professional, whose keen eye and exceptional thoroughness compensated for my deficiency in attention to detail and to Andy Steigmeier for his creative design on the cover.

My appreciation goes to my friends Janet FitzGerald, Catherine LaSasso, Chris Lanigan and Linda Arpino, whose capacity for kindness and compassion touched me deeply, especially during those difficult times.

There seem to be no words that could fully express how grateful I am to my "Mom" Haunts, who continues to so generously care for my own mother bridging the miles that stand between us.

And a special thank you to Theresa, my most loyal and treasured life-long friend.

Finally, my gratitude goes to Scott who gave me the gift of unconditional love. You were my sunshine.

Glance at the sun.

See the moon and the stars.

Gaze at the beauty of earth's greenings.

Now, think.

- Hildegard Von Bingen

Table of Contents

Preface

It was nine o'clock in the morning and I was about to lead a session on creative thinking with a large group of medical professionals. As I scanned the audience, waiting for the host to approach the podium and announce me, I overheard one of the participating physicians lean over to a colleague with evident disdain, and say "I guess you can make a cottage industry out of anything these days."

There was a time when this sort of comment would have unnerved me. Had I been a participant, I might even have said something similar if I didn't know anything about the topic. But instead, I smiled to myself with the knowledge that his attitude would change, just as mine had, as we went through the thinking techniques in the hands-on seminar.

I looked forward to witnessing his transformation, and I wasn't disappointed. His mocking tone and sarcastic comments were soon replaced by a near child-like wonder at the unexpected ideas he was developing. All it took was some concentrated effort and a little patience with learning some new thinking techniques.

Whenever people ask me what I do for a living, I tell them creative thinking and innovation, and then get ready for the pause. They often respond with "That's interesting", which is really just rhetoric for covering their skepticism. Seldom do they ask follow-up questions because people often misunderstand it as something undisciplined, unscientific or downright useless. Innovation is easily grasped, of course, but it's the creative thinking that throws people off.

If you had told me that I would be working in the field of creative thinking and innovation some day, I never would have believed it. I was an ambitious business school graduate, who took pride in my analytical thinking ability. Creative thinking was the responsibility of those graphic artist folks that I would be hiring some day.

In the way that life twists and turns, a confluence of events led me to attending a course on creative thinking more than fifteen years ago. And I confess that the only reason I attended was that someone else was paying for it and I was in need of a change of pace.

With barely a sliver of curiosity, I figured that the experience would at least have some entertainment value. Instead, it ended up changing the course of my life.

The techniques I learned helped me develop an ever-present curiosity about life and learning. They empowered me to re-frame my perspective, not because there was something wrong in the way I saw things, but because it was very limited. Possibilities began to appear where I had seen none before. I experienced a growing realization that what stopped me from seeing those possibilities, were not only the skills to think creatively, but also the boundaries that we take as truths. It was disconcerting, yet at the same time unbelievably liberating.

This book is as much about self-belief as it is about creative thinking and innovation. It is about recognizing that oftentimes, unwittingly, we are made aware of our limitations while seldom encouraged to test our boundaries or change our thinking. It is the difference between the optimist describing the glass as half full, the pessimist describing it as half empty, and the innovator saying that the glass needs re-sizing.

Ultimately, this book is about reclaiming your enthusiasm and the aliveness that accompanies novelty of thought, that characteristic that either lies in the shadow or blossoms, depending upon your life experiences and opportunities.

As a teacher at heart, I become energized when I share my learning with others and witness their surprise and delight when they find themselves thinking in ways that they never did before. It is in this spirit that I bring forth my learning to you and as you ponder the pages herein, I welcome you to share yours with me.

Introduction

She stood in the middle of the Capilano Suspension Bridge, teetering on 450 feet of swaying, wobbly, wooden slats 230 feet above rocks and fast-moving rapids in Vancouver, British Columbia, Canada. Clipboard in hand, she waited for young men to cross. And cross they did, holding on as tightly as they could.

It was certainly not a task for the faint of heart. She did this regularly over the course of a few weeks, waiting only for young men unaccompanied by women. She approached 85 men in all, telling them that she was doing research in beautiful places. She asked them a series of questions, then gave them her phone number and told them they could call if they had any follow-up questions.

If her purpose was simply to meet men, it certainly was a creative and persistent way to go about it. But that wasn't her goal; the work was part of an experiment to study attraction between the sexes. The other part of the study was a similar scenario repeated upriver by the same woman, but this time on a wide, sturdy bridge only 10 feet above a small rivulet.

What the experiment measured was the men's perceptions of the woman's attractiveness. Of the men who crossed the high, frightening bridge, about 50 percent made a follow-up call to her; of those crossing the lower one, only 12 percent did.

Scientists have known for years that attraction is likely to happen when people are aroused,[1] be it through laughter, anxiety or fear. Fear had gotten the attention of these men and alerted their brains' emotional

---

1 Schachter, S. & Singer, J.E. (1962). Cognitive, Social and Physiological Determinants of Emotional State. *Psychological Review* 69(5) 379-399.

centers. The men then attributed that arousal to the woman's presence, not to the real cause: fear.

People misattribute their feelings all the time, for a host of reasons. Unless we deem something as significant, we often just don't pay much attention to it. This is actually an example of how efficiently the brain works. It would be too taxing to pay attention to everything all the time, so we focus on the important things.

Emotions take hold of us and cause us to see the world differently. We promise to lose weight, but give in to the temptation of that chocolate dessert. We vow to save money, but that new car or outfit becomes irresistible. We promise to clean the basement, yet somehow there is always something else that we end up doing. Call it procrastination, getting sidetracked, or the need for immediate gratification, but whatever it is, we don't think too much about it.

Seldom do we think about how we think, or why we feel as we do. But being aware of both will help us understand what drives our behavior. When it comes to innovation, it is critically important to know those drivers, because that is how we develop a mindset primed for creative thinking. By simply changing your mood to a more positive one, you can broaden your view to see more possibilities and find ideas that are qualitatively richer and greater in number, even without using any thinking techniques to go further.

A serious mood will sharpen your focus to apply your analytical skills. This point is little understood, but crucially important: your mood crosses over to your thoughts so that what you feel determines how much you actually see, and one of the best ways to improve your creative thinking is to see as much as possible. This foundation must be in place before you can fully employ the creative skills necessary for thinking outside the box.

There are many paths to innovation, and this book will uncover numerous ones that are highly effective. My purpose in writing this book is to show you that creative thinking is not the sole domain of visionaries or those folks who simply march to the beat of a different drum. Creative thinking is a set of skills that can be learned and developed, and that go hand in hand with an attitude of curiosity. We are born with a curiosity that propels us to constantly ask "why?" as we interact with our environment. We start out seeing the world with fresh eyes, but as time passes, our increasing knowledge quells our inborn curiosity, and we begin to learn our limitations.

We learn the skill of logic, which is both our friend and our nemesis. It is our friend because it helps us make decisions, and yet it is our nemesis because it prematurely filters our thinking. Seeds of ideas exist everywhere, but to recognize them we need to hold back the judgment spoken by common sense. They are only seeds because they are not fully functioning ideas. They need growth, refinement, and development.

This is perhaps one of the most under-estimated, misunderstood concepts of creative thinking, particularly in the corporate world today. When seeds of ideas and whole ideas are lumped, some end up being quickly dismissed because they do not pass the criteria of logic and reason. We rush too hastily to judgment.

The essence of creative thinking is holding your mind open long enough to entertain those possibilities of thinking you normally would not. These are the seeds of ideas that are not logical, cost-effective or strategically aligned.

Imagine the spectrum of creative thinking as a line. At the left side is an idea that is mundane, but logical and doable. By continually making improvements you can develop it into something better.

Moving along the continuum, for example, you can increase the number of flavors to a cereal, add new shapes to a product's packaging, and build efficiency by streamlining processes. These are examples of the continuous improvement initiative spawned by Dr. W. Edwards Deming, known as the father of the Japanese post-war industrial revival. He helped Japanese manufacturers shift from making cheap imitations to making innovative, high-quality products at the end of World War II by making continual improvements.

Japan, of course, is now regarded as a world leader in quality goods. That is a necessary part of remaining competitive. But it's not the end of the story: Japan's competitors also develop high-quality goods. And your competitors, too, are developing quality; top quality is now commoditized and is now the entry ticket to the competitive playing field. Quality is expected.

The question, then, is how do you differentiate yourselves from your competitors to gain a sustainable competitive advantage? In a word: creativity.

This is where the other side of the creativity spectrum comes into focus. Instead of starting small inside and building out, we start outside and come back in. We start with the illogical, unfinished ideas outside the box of reason, and mine them for seeds of ideas.

Be aware that it's not easy. Judgment sits in wait, ready to pounce like a lion on its prey. Entertaining illogical thoughts puts us into a zone of discomfort that builds tension as we try to make sense of those thoughts. It's usually a relief when we are snapped back to reason.

But this book will give you techniques to overcome that discomfort and erase the tension, thereby allowing you to think freely and creatively.

In Part One, chapters 1 through 3, you will get underneath your thinking to be more aware of what caused you to think in the ways that you do. We will examine the obstacles to thinking creatively, and also the ways your emotions affect your thinking. We will look at some of the subtle factors that cause you to make decisions of which you are not even aware; once you understand this, you won't ever be fooled by them again. All of these set you up to more fully appreciate chapter 4 where the concept of boundary becomes vastly porous.

In chapters 5 and 6 we continue with our heightened observations, but now we cast our sights toward a little-known emerging body of knowledge, inspired by nature, where examples of innovation literally surround us, inviting imitation and replication. This discovery shows us how we have been seeing for a long time, but not really noticing the enormous lessons before us.

In Part Two, chapters 7 through 14, we focus on active thinking techniques, exploring a host of different tools that will challenge your current thinking style. These creative thinking strategies have led others to "game-changing" innovations, and will open up for you your ability to recognize seeds of ideas where you never saw them before.

In Part Three, chapters 15 through 21, you will be inspired by some innovators who have significantly changed our world for the better, despite facing incredible obstacles. Their stories remind us that no matter what the nature of an innovation is, complex or simple, we all have the capacity to innovate. By reading this book and absorbing its ideas, you will have the tools to innovate.

The innovator sees the same world you do, but sees more. This book will foster the deep curiosity that fades when we leave childhood, so that the taken-for-granted will not be taken for granted any longer.

Throughout this book you will engage in thought experiments that will expand the current limits of your thinking. In essence, this book will change the way you think. As Oliver Wendell Holmes once said, "A mind once stretched by a new idea never regains its original dimension." After you read this, you will not see the world in the same way that you did before, and there will be no turning back. But as you experience the journey of increasing mental freedom, you won't want to.

Part One

Chapter 1

Imagination and Knowledge

Picture a young man, holding a mirror in one hand and staring at his reflection, and in the other hand pointing a flashlight toward his face so he is looking at himself lit up. He is, apparently, quite engrossed. You have been watching him do this for several minutes.

What would you think? If this was a young child, you wouldn't think too much about it. Children experiment all the time as they explore their environments, so they sometimes do strange things. But this behavior is odd for an adult. You might think that this man is narcissistic, so taken is he with his image, or you might simply dismiss him as "not all there" and give him little thought.

Well, there was such a man, and many thought him to be strange. The American F.B.I. kept a 1,427-page file on his activities[2] and recommended that he be barred from immigrating to the United States under the Alien Exclusion Act. He was a German citizen, and the F.B.I. alleged that he "believed in, advised, advocated, or taught a doctrine which, in a legal sense, as held by the courts in other cases, 'would allow anarchy to stalk in unmolested.'" They were referring, of course, to his involvement with the Communist Party in the early 1900s.

Indeed, something seemed to be amiss with this man, but political affiliations aside, just what was he doing staring into mirrors while lighting his face?

---

2   Albert Einstein, 1,427 pages. Retrieved February 19, 2009 from http://foia.fbi.gov/foiaindex/einstein.html.

Deep in thought, he was imagining himself riding on a beam of light across the universe and back, wondering about the speed of light and how it related to the concept of time. His name was Albert Einstein and these strange behaviors led to his Theory of Relativity.

As Einstein often pointed out, "Imagination is more important than knowledge."

Einstein was regarded as one of the most brilliant mathematical physicists of the century, although he considered himself as much a philosopher as a scientist. This is a critical point in understanding how breakthrough thinking occurs.

A common misunderstanding of science is this: scientists are unbiased observers who use the scientific method to confirm or disprove various theories. Further, it is thought, scientists collect data objectively, then logically derive theories from their data. Logic will determine what is true or untrue, and right or wrong, because it is the scientific method. According to this line of thinking, science has no other method; this is how knowledge is formed.

This sounds impressive, but it is almost completely untrue.

Data cannot conclusively confirm or falsify theories because it is quite subjective in practice. Scientists, moreover, have been known to defend their theories in the face of conflicting data. The fact is that science is subjective. Further, philosophizing is just as important as observing, measuring and analyzing, when information is being sought or theories are being formed. But as Einstein said, knowledge is limited to all we now know and understand. Logic will take you from A to B, but imagination will take you everywhere. It is imagination that causes you to explore new territories in thinking.

In the corporate world, letting your imagination run away with you is generally frowned upon. If you come up with a new idea, you had better not share it unless you also have a full cost-benefit analysis and, in addition, can show how the idea fits within the company's time-honored customs.

There are also social psychological principles at work that inhibit the sharing of fresh thinking. We are hired for our intelligence, and in our efforts to succeed, we avoid any actions or statements that might compromise others' perceptions about us. Moreover, if one person debunks another's ideas, it may often appear, perhaps wrongly, that the one doing the criticizing is more intelligent than the one being criticized, because the critical person saw something others did not. And if the criticism is delivered articulately, well, that's even more impressive.

When the radio was introduced in 1865, an editorial in the Boston Post read: "*Well informed people know it is impossible to transmit the voice over wires and that were it possible to do so, the thing would be of no practical value. We have plenty of small boys to run messages.*" When an idea or concept is new, it is easier to see why it won't work than why it will.

There are other inhibiting forces at work that are subtle, yet no less powerful. Consider this situation. Imagine being called into a meeting with the boss and about 12 colleagues where you asked to take part in an informal focus group. Your company makes pet food and supplies. One of your marketing specialists is asking for your reaction to a television ad on a new product. You see a video with three dogs ready to run a race side by side. The camera films from above as each dog eats a certain brand of food shown by the label on his or her collar. Your brand is on the collar of Dog No. 2. The music builds into a crescendo, the starting gun goes off, and they bound out of the gate.

Once the race is over, the marketing specialist asks each of you to state which dog won. Dog No. 2 won. You're next to last among the group in the room. Everyone before you says Dog No. 2. You say Dog

No. 2. It's obvious, the implication being that your dog won because your food is the most nutritious.

You then see a second video, this one with three cats. This time the cats are chasing a mechanical mouse on a track. As in the previous video, each cat eats a specific brand of food, with your brand attached to Cat No. 3. The music starts, the gate opens, and the cats chase the mouse around the track. Cat No. 3 wins. You are asked which cat won. It's indisputable, and you begin to wonder why you're even being asked this. Everyone says Cat No. 3, and so do you.

You are now asked to view a third video. This time there are turtles lined up at a gate, with your brand attached to Turtle No. 1. It's the same scenario: Music plays, gate opens -- but this time, the turtles go in different directions and, of course, very slowly.

When the race is over, only one turtle, No. 3, has advanced a few steps ahead in a direct line, while Turtle No. 1 and Turtle No. 2 are at the sidelines. You are asked which won.

At first you think this must be a joke, but no one is laughing. You start to feel a little annoyed by this infringement on your time and would normally look for a way to leave the room as soon as possible. But what happens next rivets you to your chair. One by one, each person says that Turtle No.1 (the one with your brand) won the race. You look back at the screen to see if you missed something, but the closing shot clearly indicates that Turtle No.1 is on the sideline. Even your boss says that Turtle No.1 was the winner, and no one is looking askance. Everyone says it with a straight face. Now it's your turn.

What will you say?

Will you tell the truth and say it is Turtle No. 3? Or will you say that it was Turtle No. 1, the one with your brand name on its back, that won the race?

Believe it or not, there is a two-thirds chance that you would agree with everyone else that Turtle No. 1 won the race. You wouldn't really change your opinion, but you would say that you agree.

The reason is this: the need for social approval is stronger than the need to be right.[3] It is more important to protect your self-esteem. For this reason, even when people know that what they are doing is wrong, more often than not they will go along anyway to avoid feeling peculiar or appearing to be a fool. Decades of research have illustrated this powerful norm even when the situations have involved complete strangers.[4] This is the principle of normative social influence.

This experiment helps explain why so much creativity is dampened in the corporate world. Our self-esteem and our needs for social approval, for protection and acceptance, run counter to the risk and rejection of new ideas that form part of the creative process.

It is indeed risky to share unsubstantiated thoughts, what-ifs and illogical ponderings, in essence, the stuff creative thinking is about.

How do you make a safe environment for people to share and explore new territories of thinking? With the best of intentions, managers often announce the ground rules of brain-storming sessions, the first being that all ideas are good ideas. It is a good start, but it's not enough, because people will still, understandably, filter what they say. People know that even if a criticism is not uttered, it is thought, and too often evidenced, by a rolling of the eyes or an awkward silence. Even worse is the feeling of

---

3   Ash, S.E. (1955). Opinions and Social Pressure. *Scientific American, 193* http://www. panarchy.org/asch/social pressure,1955 html.
4   Moscovi, S. (1966). Social Influence and Conformity. *Handbook of Social Psychology.* New York: McGraw-Hill 347-412 (Eds.) G. Lindzey & E. Aronson, and Bond, R. and Smith, P. Culture and Conformity: A Meta-Analysis of Studies Using Asch's (1952, 1956) Line Judgment Task. *Psychological Bulletin, 119.* 111-137

sharing an imaginative idea, only to find that it doesn't get written on the flip-chart when all others did.

There are many ways to turn imaginative and impractical thoughts into workable ideas, but first one must indulge in the imaginative world of fantasy without constraint. It is the important precursor to this rich process. You cannot perceive if you cannot conceive.

In working with groups, a few pointers to enhance the brainstorming process are:

1. Invite people from diverse backgrounds to get a diversity of perspectives;

2. Hold the session in the morning when people are fresh and relatively unencumbered by the events of the day;

3. Invite people with a sense of humor. They are the ones who will break the ice, get people to relax and through their jokes and one-liners, cause people to see things from a different perspective and thereby get others to explore new territories of thinking.[5]

4. Follow these guidelines:

   (a) You have all the money in the world.

   (b) You don't have to explain <u>how</u> an idea works. Just explain <u>what</u> it is.

   (c) Be playful. The more extreme the idea, the better.

5. Make it known that quantity of ideas is more important than quality. The more you have, the more you have to work with.

---

5   See page 40 for a full explanation of how humor enhances creative thinking.

Quality comes later. In explaining how scientific theories are created, the Nobel Prize-winning chemist Linus Pauling maintained that one must try to come up with as many ideas as possible and then discard the useless ones. Just do not be too quick to discard. As you have seen, even wild ideas may be seeds of value, which can only become obvious if they are developed further.

6. Find what works in a fantastic idea, not what doesn't. See below.

Remember that what begins in the mind ends up in physical reality. Leonardo da Vinci, the great painter, sculptor and inventor, was known for his imaginings. He drew his visions of the airplane, the helicopter, the parachute, the submarine and the car more than 300 years before they became reality. You may not rival Leonardo for his prescience, but you can allow yourself to imagine without evaluating whether your thoughts are realistic or not. We are too often deceived by our own opinions; we have learned what works and what does not from today's reality. But today's musings can be tomorrow's reality.

An essential component of the process is to illustrate how fantasies are used as stepping-stones to practical ideas. The trick is to look for something positive in that fantastic idea, rather than rejecting it for its flaws.

For example, in a focus group sponsored by a travel company, some business travelers were complaining about the hassles of travel today, with extra security checks, long lines at airports, and long hours of inactivity during flights.

They were then asked to imagine their perfect worlds: If they could enhance the travel experience on the plane, what would they change? "Assume the plane is so wonderful that you want to get on it and never get off," the focus group leader urged them. This suggestion fast-tracks the participants to think of the ultimate experience, rather than the simply new and slightly improved. The ideas began to flow.

"I want a plane that has all the amenities. A chef, a dining room, a wide-screen television, my own living room and an exercise room."

"Just let me play golf, so I can relax and perfect my score. I want to get off the plane more relaxed than when I got on."

"I'd like an Olympic-size swimming pool where I can swim laps."

"I want an Xtreme Makeover to look like a famous Hollywood actress by the time I get off."

The first fantasy is already becoming a reality. The new Airbus 380 has mini-hotel suites, each with a double bed and living area with a wide-screen television that can serve as your dining room. There is a choice of meals on demand. The chefs may not be on board, but you can read about them in your menu.

There is plenty of room to exercise. It is not a separate exercise room, but rather a case in which we take a piece of that idea and say: "If we cannot provide a room to exercise, what other ways can we provide exercise options?" All you need is a little space for calisthenics, and with 50 percent more floor space on this plane, you have it. The airline could simply provide a menu of suggested exercises as an inexpensive value-added service.

The second fantasy needs more manipulation, because a golf course surpasses space constraints. So we cannot offer it literally, in its totality, but we can provide it in smaller pieces. Portable putting greens are inexpensive. The airline could provide one, with a choice of instructional wii game consoles to allow people to practice just about anything from their golf swings to yoga.

Extracting smaller pieces, or seeds, from the whole idea applies to the Olympic-sized swimming pool as well. What can we take from this fantasy? We can provide hot steamed towels with a beauty consultant to provide facials, or a mini-stall for showers using water-saving showerheads.

And what about the Xtreme Makeover? Make it less extreme, but offer mini-makeovers. An esthetician can be onboard to give makeovers and spa-type services. A new haircut may not make you look like a Hollywood star, but it can make you feel like as new person!

Extra services can always be offered at a premium, of course. But you might be wondering about economy class -- these ideas will clearly not work there. But just try to follow the same line of thinking and ask how you can take a piece of the idea and make it work in a smaller way to fit the budget constraints. If you cannot do that, ask what the benefits of the fantasy idea were and then try to achieve them in a similar, less costly way.

Exercise: Stepping Stones

Suppose that you are looking for ideas to make your commuting to and from work less arduous. Every day you sit in traffic in your car. What can you do? Carpooling, bicycling, walking and flextime are current practices to help alleviate the problem so we won't consider these unless we enhance them in some way. Start by listing some fantasy ideas that you do not expect to happen in column 1. Then in column 2 list some benefits for each fantasy. Now in column 3 come up with some ideas to achieve those benefits in smaller ways.

One	Two	Three
Fantasy	Benefits of Fantasy	Smaller Ideas to Achieve Benefits
No commuting at all	Extra time to get work done and get home every day.	The company provides vans equipped with office equipment so you can start your work day as soon as you get in. The van picks you and your co-workers up who live in your geographic area at the actual time you would be at work so you could leave your house later in the morning and leave earlier at the end of the day.
See friends and have fun instead of commuting.	Work less and have more fun in my life every day.	Once or twice a week vanpool with others and play games or see films in serial times to fit into your commute time.
Learn a new hobby or skill instead of commute?	?	?
?	?	?

By following this stepping stone-method, you will avoid rejecting the whole idea and instead see the many seeds within, each with its own merits. This is a giant leap to unleashing your thinking potential.

I like nonsense, it wakes up the brain cells. Fantasy is a necessary ingredient in living, it's a way of looking at life through the wrong end of a telescope. Which is what I do, and that enables you to laugh at life's realities.
Theodore Geisel
a.k.a. Dr. Seuss

Chapter 2

Thinking About Thinking

The dinner was going well between Ed and Cindy, who were on their second date. Romantic restaurant, delicious food, good bottle of wine and lots of conversation. It was getting late, and Ed suggested that Cindy join him for a nightcap at his place, which was right around the corner. "I'd love to," she said, aware of the fact that she was already a bit tipsy, but thinking that she hadn't had this much fun in a long time. So off they went.

The conversation continued to be delightful, and Cindy basked in all the attention Ed was giving her. The looks they exchanged were becoming longer, and were followed by suppressed smiles expressing a deep attraction that neither could deny. Reluctant to break this wonderful floating feeling, Cindy had to excuse herself to use the bathroom. *Could it be that she'd finally met the one?* she wondered as she made her way there, swaying a bit from the effects of the wine.

Leaning over the sink to wash her hands, she spied a bottle of prescription pills on the counter. Always respectful of another's privacy, she prided herself on being curious but not nosey. She smiled to herself as she washed her hands with soap and water. Yes, she thought, she would resist the temptation to look. She was better than that. The fact that she was employed as a pharmaceutical sales representative was even greater testament to her self control.

She leaned over a little more than necessary to get the towel to dry her hands. What a coincidence that she could see the label on the bottle! The slight pang of guilt she felt was erased with a jolt when she read it. She couldn't remember exactly what it was for, but she knew for certain that she had seen this drug in every institution where she supplied anti-psychotic medications. Her mind raced as she frantically tried to recall what this drug was for. Could it be that this lovely man was psychotic? Sobriety came crashing in and her thoughts raced.

It all began to make sense now. His delayed responses. His way of staring back at her with glassy eyes, saying nothing at times. His keen interest in what she did for a living. He wasn't shy, she realized now. These were some of the side effects associated with those powerful drugs. How could she have missed this? But, she wondered, how could he have a responsible job and nice house? The stupidity of her assumptions hit her hard. Job? House? She had blindly taken his word on those. There was no proof of either.

Fear, panic and embarrassment were all rolled up into one. She was trapped in the bathroom of a psychopath, and all because of her own stupidity. Thoughts of escape mingled with visions of fighting for her life. Thank goodness her nails were long, she thought. She could scratch him hard so that the DNA would provide evidence to the police in their investigation later. "Get a grip," she said to herself, knowing that her thoughts were irrational, but also feeling her fear building into terror. So this was how it was going to end. She took a deep breath. She had to keep herself together if she had any chance of escape.

With all the self-control she could muster, Cindy opened the bathroom door and walked back to the living room where Ed was waiting. She forced a brief smile, hoping fervently that he could not see the fear beneath. Her purse was at the edge of the couch with her car keys inside. All she had to do was grab it and run. If only she could distract him somehow to get a head start. She could not fail, because there would be no second chance. "That's a very interesting book," she said, pointing in the general direction of the bookcase. "When did you read it?" she asked, conscious of the slight shakiness of her voice.

As he turned to look, Cindy grabbed her purse, ran down the hallway and burst through the door. As she ran, she could hear Ed calling after her. She jumped into the driver's seat and screeched away from the curb, nearly giddy with relief as the tears began to run down her cheeks.

Soon afterward, exhausted, she arrived home and immediately pulled the Physician's Desk Reference, the handbook of all manufactured pharmaceuticals, off her bookshelf, to see what those pills were for. She would now learn about the danger she had narrowly escaped. It said *"Allopurinol ... used to treat gout and certain types of kidney stones ...."* She read it again, to be sure, and embarrassment began to seep into her consciousness. Ed's only affliction, besides choosing a heedless woman to date that night, was a mild form of arthritis!

Explaining one's way out of an incident like this would require creativity unto itself. It took a few weeks for Cindy to approach Ed. With time's softening effect and Ed's ability to recognize the humor in the situation, that unlikely turn of events led to a thoughtful conversation; a year later, the two married. The incident was an unforgettable lesson to Cindy about jumping to conclusions.

It can happen to the best of us. Daniel Goleman, the author of the seminal book called Emotional Intelligence, calls it the amygdala hijack.[6] It occurs when our emotions take hold and we react before we have time to think. The amygdala is a part of the brain responsible for mediating emotions, and it can take over the rational part of the brain when there is perceived danger, whether that danger is real or not.

---

6   A term coined by Daniel Goleman (1995) in his groundbreaking book *Emotional Intelligence.* New York: Bantam Books

The amygdala launches the fight or flight response and forces us into dichotomous, all-or-nothing thinking, making it easier to jump to conclusions, as Cindy did.

Under the circumstances, Cindy can be excused for not thinking enough about how she was thinking. But what happens in situations where we are not emotionally hijacked and, in fact, feeling cool-headed? Do we think about how we think?

This is what cognitive psychologists call 'metacognition' – thinking about how we think.

But do we do this? Not much, it appears. Thinking is something we just do unless, of course, you practice meditation. Then you work at controlling your conscious thoughts and become more mindful of your thinking.

Metacognition is important because it helps us to achieve the freedom of thinking that fuels creativity. There are many factors that compromise our thinking, albeit in subtle ways. While we do not typically face physical danger in our day-to-day lives, we do face the stress of time pressures, especially in a competitive global environment. Thinking is hard work and it takes time. Whatever we can do to understand how we think, and to sort through the barrage of information we face every day to make decisions efficiently, is helpful.

Sorting information into dichotomies helps. They enable us to simplify our thinking by distilling information into its' essence, or bare minimum, saving us the time to think it over. That helps us get a lot accomplished, but at the cost of shortchanging ourselves because it becomes a filter that halts the creative process before it has even begun.

Here's what often happens: An idea is offered and immediately we judge its merit. Is it logical? Does it make sense? Will it make us money? Is it worth doing? Yes? Accept it. No? Reject it. There is no middle ground. In the same way that Cindy overlooked other cues that would have affirmed positive qualities about Ed, we do not consider all of the potential benefits to an idea. We look for the diamonds, not the diamonds in the rough.

This often happens because we avoid ambiguity. We have a need for closure because uncertainty is uncomfortable. Studies on creativity, in fact, have shown that individuals who rate lower on a measure of need for closure produced a larger number of novel solutions and were generally more productive and creative.[7]

Another detractor from thinking freely and creatively is one that impacts you as a consumer, and therefore, your wallet, almost every day. It is very clever because it affects your thoughts, ideas and decision-making, and you are probably not even aware of it. It is the use of decoys.[8] We might think that we make decisions in absolute terms, but we do not. Most decisions are made relative to one another. Dan Ariely, Professor of Behavioral Economics at Duke University, illustrates this in the following example:

The Economist magazine ran a subscription ad, inviting people to pick their subscription or renewal from this list:

Economist.com subscription - $59

One-year subscription to Economist.com. Includes online access to all articles from The Economist since 1997.

7 Chirumbolo, A., Livi, St., Mannetti, L., Pierro, A., Kruglanski, A.W. (2004). Effects of Need for Closure On Creativity In Small Group Interactions." *European Journal of Personality 18* 265-278

8 Ariely, D. (2008). *Predictably Irrational: The Hidden Forces That Shape Our Decisions.* New York: Harper Collins Publishers.

Print subscription - $125

One-year subscription to the print edition of The Economist.

Print and web subscription - $125

One-year subscription to the print edition of The Economist and online access to all articles from The Economist since 1997.

It is clear that the third option is better than the second one because you get both the web and print options. You don't have to think too hard to decide between those two. Deciding between the first option, web-only access, or the second option, print-only access, takes more thinking with the price difference, and thinking is hard work. The folks at The Economist do not want you to think too much about it, but they do want to make money, so they want you to go for the more expensive option. That is why choice number two is added as an option. It is intended to sway you to the third option. It is the decoy.

Ariely did an experiment with 100 students to see if this held true. He found that 16 students chose the web-only subscription for $59, not one chose the print-only subscription, and 84 students chose the print-and-web option for $125.

To test the decoy theory, Ariely repeated the study and offered the students only two possibilities: the web-only choice at $59 and the print-and-web choice at $125. The results differed: 68 students chose the web-only option, while 32 chose the print-and-web option. The absence of the decoy showed that now the print-and-web option was not as appealing, because the option that could be compared directly with it was removed. This is an effective illustration of how we use relativity.

Now think of how often this can be employed to influence your decisions. For example, you want to go on a vacation. Your choices are:

St. Lucia, 7 nights with airfare, accommodation and water activities (such as Scuba, snorkeling, jet skiing) $1,199

St. Maarten, 6 nights with airfare, accommodation, but no water activities for $1,299

St. Maarten, 7 nights with airfare, accommodation and water activities for $1,299

If you were looking only for some sun and relaxation on the beach, then the choice between St. Lucia and St. Maarten would require some thought, as they are very similar. With the addition of the decoy option of St. Maarten with airfare, accommodation and no water activities, the third option is sweetened.

The decoy effect is at work in more ways than you can imagine. You frequently see restaurant menus with a high-priced item, the decoy. It is not expected that you will order this item, but its presence makes the second highest priced item more appealing.[9]

Although not a decoy in itself, your decisions are manipulated when you are offered an added choice, relative to the first. When you order a burger for $3.25 for example, and the waiter asks if you want fries for only $1.00 more, you have experienced a decoy-like effect. When you are buying a car and the salesperson says you can have a sunroof for only $150 more, it has happened again. This manipulative tactic can be found anywhere from how much you get paid to whom you marry.

---

9   ibid.

So what is the message here? It is this: Our thinking is not as clear and unbiased as we might think. Time, stress, ambiguity and manipulations such as decoys, all affect the quality of our thinking, and that can impact our ability to think more creatively.

Thinking about how we think can help us get beyond the limitations and biases imposed by others, effectively helping us to think outside the box. Increasing your mindfulness about these factors can help you take control of your thinking. In fact, you might even consider using the decoy effect yourself to persuade others of the benefit of your ideas because new ideas, as we all know, almost always face resistance.

Exercise: Spot the Decoy

Decoy?

Scenario 1: You are shopping for a briefcase and you see three that you like.
Briefcase # 1 is black leather, with an outside pocket, shoulder strap and costs $450.00. The 2nd briefcase is the same size and also has an outside pocket and shoulder strap, but is made of canvas. It costs $150.00.
The 3rd briefcase is the same size with no outside pocket, but has a shoulder strap. It is made of black leather and costs $450.00. Which one is the decoy?

Briefcase # 1 made of black leather, with an outside pocket and shoulder strap that costs $450.00

_____

Briefcase # 2 made of canvas, same size with an outside pocket, but with shoulder strap. It costs $150.00

———————

Briefcase # 3 made of black leather, with no outside pocket, but has a shoulder strap, costing $450.00

———————

Scenario 2: Your spouse suggests going out for dinner to a restaurant that is 20 minutes away. You want to go out, but you don't want to drive that far, so you suggest going to a restaurant that is just down the street. Your spouse then suggests going to yet another restaurant that is 45 minutes away. Which one is the decoy?

The restaurant 20 minutes away.

———————

The restaurant just down the street.

———————

The restaurant that is 45 minutes away.

———————

Answers:

Scenario 1: Briefcase # 3 is the decoy. It makes briefcase # 1 more attractive because it has the outside pocket for the same price.

Scenario # 2: The restaurant 45 minutes away is the decoy. While it is not as convenient as your choice of restaurant down the street, it makes your spouse's first choice of a restaurant 20 minutes away seem more acceptable.

Chapter 3

The Connection Between Emotional Intelligence and Creative Thinking

From the get-go, the meeting did not go well. The mood was somber and, though there were relatively few people, the formality was stifling. It was a strategic planning meeting of the executive team of a building products company, and those attending were the C.E.O., Eric; his 10 vice-presidents; and an outside consultant, Amanda. Amanda, an innovation consultant, was there to facilitate the session and guide the others in expanding their thinking and generating new ideas.

Before the meeting, Eric had called to confide that there seemed to be a morale problem in the company, even though market conditions were quite good. His meetings with the division heads were often characterized by a sort of malaise, he said, although he couldn't put his finger on it. At their level, they should be showing some motivation about their work and setting a better example of leadership to their direct reports. If they weren't excited about their work, how could anyone else be? He knew they were a talented group, but suspected that their apparent lack of energy meant they were not working to their potential. Could she help motivate and excite them in getting some new ideas to move the business forward, he asked. "Of course," she said. Creative thinking was her specialty.

A few days before the meeting Amanda called each of the vice presidents to get some background on their divisions and general information that would help her in running the meeting. What became clear in the conversations was that these vice presidents considered Eric to be brilliant. Not just smart, but brilliant. Some had described him as a hard-driving manager who demanded results. Yes, he was critical at times. He didn't suffer fools gladly, but everyone knew that he was quite a visionary. Like him or hate him, they said, you had to respect him.

The meeting was now underway and Amanda wondered why everyone was so quiet? The awkwardness was palpable. It was now time for her to jump in and lead the session. Mustering all her energy, she injected a little more enthusiasm into her voice to add some life to the dull atmosphere. That didn't help.

What did help was her decision to stand at the front of the room, giving her a better vantage point from which to observe the group and watch their facial expressions. After only a few minutes, the problem was clear, and she understood that it was about to make her job a lot tougher.

Every time she made a light comment designed to elicit a chuckle or two, she saw the team members' look sideways toward Eric. No one laughed unless Eric laughed. When she posed a question, no one said anything without a furtive glance toward Eric first. They seemed to need at least his tacit approval before they uttered a word. His demeanor, serious and somewhat aloof, didn't help the dynamics, and more important, neither did what his direct reports had described as his 'brilliance'.

When the group was asked for ideas, and one of the V.P.'s suggested an unusual idea, Eric asked incredulously, "Where did you get that idea from?" The question was clearly rhetorical, requiring no response, and the heavy sarcasm was evident in his tone.

Another suggestion was proffered by Jim, another one of the V.P.'s, and this time, Eric simply looked away. The grimace on his face communicated disgust. In a measured tone, Eric then said: "For those of you who actually read the market trend study I sent out last week, did you understand it?" A couple of people shifted in their seats, looking down to avoid Eric's glare. The tension was excruciating. It was evident that the problem was Eric.

People naturally place more significance on what the most powerful person says and does, and a leader's emotional tone has a powerful effect on a group. Eric's seriousness was bringing down the group, and his critical comments undermined the others. Exacerbating this was the perception of his brilliance. He intimidated others and cast a tall shadow as a leader.

If you work with someone more senior than you, whom you regard as brilliant, and that person criticizes your ideas often, it can torpedo your sense of self-confidence. We all have a need to be valued and to be perceived as intelligent. While Eric himself didn't understand it, his negativity and his remarks about his subordinates' lack of intelligence were demoralizing and demotivating them. He was right in his suspicion that his team was not working to their potential, but he had no idea that he was the cause.

In innovation, attitude is just as important as aptitude, and setting the right tone to foster creative thinking is crucial. Researchers have found that mood has a direct effect on thinking abilities.

In a series of experiments, researchers manipulated subjects' moods by showing them films that would elicit various emotions. Some of the subjects saw positive films with comedy, others saw negative films on Nazi concentration camps, and the rest saw neutral films.[10] They were then asked to solve a task that required some creative thinking ability. Results found that those in the group who saw positive films were more likely to find a creative solution than were those who saw the negative or neutral films.

---

10 Isen, A., Daubman, K. and Nowicki, G. (1998). Positive Affect Facilitates Creative Problem Solving. In (Eds.) J. M. Jenkins and K. Oatley. *Human Emotions: A Reader.* (pp. 270-287). New York: Blackwell Publishers, Inc.

A positive mood is associated with a greater expansiveness of thinking, opening up one's perceptual landscape to a broader array of potential solutions in the problem-solving process. A negative mood, on the other hand, is associated with a narrower, more focused approach, manifesting a greater attention to detail. If the focus of this meeting was to simply review detailed information, then Eric might have primed the group toward greater accuracy, but his hurtful insinuations inhibited any potential for creative thinking.

The crossover of mood and thinking, of course, extends beyond the creative thinking session; emotions are enduring, sometimes lasting over a period of many years. Occurring just below the level of consciousness, these covert emotions can direct our behaviors in ways that we misunderstand simply because we have forgotten their beginnings.

Dr. Antonio Damasio, a professor of neurology at the University of Southern California, explains the nature of covert emotion in the case of David, a patient with a severe defect in learning and memory, who cannot learn any new fact at all.[11] David could not learn any new sound or place or any new physical appearance, rendering him incapable of learning to recognize any new person from the face, voice or name, or anything at all about the events that may have transpired between him and that person. This severe deficit was caused by extensive damage to David's hippocampus, a region in the brain that is responsible for creating memories for new facts, and another area called the amygdala, responsible for mediating emotion.

David clearly displayed consistent preferences and avoidances for certain people. He would go to specific people in the facility where he lived for a cigarette or a cup of coffee; there were some people to whom

---

11   Damasio, A. *The Feeling of What Happens: Body And Emotion in The Making of Consciousness.* Florida: Harcourt, Inc.,1999.

he would never go. This was most intriguing given the fact that he did not recognize any of those individuals. Damasio and Tranel, a Professor of Psychology and Neurology, at the University of Iowa College of Medicine, conducted an experiment to find out why. They called it the good-guy/bad-guy experiment.[12] Over the course of a week, they had David engage with three distinct types of people: first, those who were extremely pleasant and who always rewarded David, whether he requested something or not; second, a person who was emotionally neutral and engaged David in activities that were neither pleasant or unpleasant; and a third person whose manner was brusque, who would refuse all of David's requests, and who engaged him in tedious psychological tasks.

All interactions were staged so that each type had equal exposure in a random order. Afterward, the experimenters asked David to look at sets of four photographs that included the face of one of the individuals in the experiment. They then asked David, "Whom would you go to if you needed help?" and "Who do you think is your friend in this group?"

More than 80 percent of the time, David chose the person who had been good to him, clearly indicating that that his choice was not random. The neutral person was not chosen with any probability greater than chance, and the negative person was almost never chosen.

When David was asked to tell the experimenters what he knew about the people behind the photographs, he could not remember ever encountering them or any the events during that experiment. David did not know why he chose one person over the other. It was a nonconscious preference he manifested, these experimenters suggest, that is most likely related to the emotions that the experiment called forth. Something had

---

12   Tranel, D. and Damasio, A. "The Cover Learning of Affective Valence Does of Require Structures in Hippocampal System or Amygdala." *Journal of Cognitive Neuroscience* 5 (1993): 79-88.

remained in his brain that caused him to behave in ways that matched the emotional power of the original encounters.

Interestingly, Damasio said that, when David was being led into the experiment room and spotted the bad guy, he flinched, stopped for an instant, then allowed himself to be led into the room. Asked what was the matter, David told him that everything was all right as nothing came to mind. As Damasio explains, the bad guy induced a brief emotional response and a brief here-and-now feeling, but without the associated set of images to suggest the cause of his reaction, and so the effect on David remained isolated and disconnected.

This study illustrates how central emotions are to our everyday thinking and highlights the importance of paying attention to them when dealing with others. I am not suggesting, nor is it reasonable to expect, that we should always strive to be the "good guys", but it is reasonable to expect leaders to be aware of how their leadership style is affecting others in the present and over time. They can either help or hinder the creative process and to a larger extent, the motivation of others, by understanding the characteristics that facilitate each.

We feel many things through the course of a day, and often we are unaware of the cause, which may have simply been an image, a scent, the weather, or the state of your health. Regardless of what we feel, though, we can control the expression of those emotions to affect others' behaviors and avoid being a roadblock to creative thinking.

When you think of the many inherent hurdles to thinking creatively, especially in the corporate world where hierarchies are followed, it is a wonder that creative thinking happens at all. One particular hurdle that is subtle, yet potent, is our need to be perceived as intelligent.

What better opportunity to show others how intelligent we are than to criticize another's ideas in a meeting? The better you can de-bunk another's viewpoints, the smarter people think you are, especially if your criticism is articulate. A serious demeanor, moreover, can reinforce an impression of thoughtfulness even if it is totally false.

If you do this often enough, and if you are right some of the time, people may even regard you as brilliant. Then the intimidation begins. People pull back when you cast the shadow of brilliance, real or not, and when that happens, their talents, abilities and intelligence become harder to see.

An environment conducive to getting the best thinking from a team requires open communication and ensuring that everyone gets heard. When you satisfy a person's need to be heard, it is a sign of respect, and that encourages them to speak more freely. Add an upbeat tone to foster some camaraderie and you can begin to dissolve some of the other interpersonal barriers that can get in the way of productive conversations.

But in some sessions, intimidation takes place. Sometimes a person's strengths can intimidate others, especially when those others feel that they don't measure up. Intelligence, beauty, articulateness and any of the obvious accoutrements of success such as title or rank, and wealth, can cause intimidation, stirring up others' insecurities.

Everyone feels insecurities from time to time and they are part of human nature. The savvy person who connects with others easily is the person who is aware of her effect on others, and adapts her behaviors accordingly. It does not mean that they must change who they are. For instance, a strong leader may need to pull back in meetings and ask more questions rather than make statements so that others will come forward.

The connection between emotional intelligence, particularly mood, and creative thinking was further explored by these researchers to determine if it was positive mood by itself that expands thinking abilities.

They conducted a variation of this study using a candy bar to induce a positive mood. The results differed. This time the group showed no improvement in performance. So the question now is, what was missing in the candy bar study that was present in the comedic film study? The missing ingredient was humor.

As the creative thinking guru, de Bono once said, humor is by far the most significant behavior of the human brain. It opens up new pathways of thinking because it requires you to go from one track of thinking to another, from the linear, connected thought process to another, seemingly unrelated thought, when you hear the punch line. It is what enables you to shift perspective to look at things in a different light. Listening to a joke is a good example of this. You hear the punch line, and for a brief moment, you pause. Then aha, you get the connection and (hopefully) laugh. It is an example of a new connection in thinking, and that, in essence, is a definition of creative thinking.

In the situation with Eric, no amount of humor could undo the damage he had done to the team dynamic. Fortunately, Amanda knew this and changed the plan. She called a break, took Eric outside, told him briefly that he was part of the problem and asked him to leave for a couple of hours. She instructed him to come back with a snorkel, rubber duck or anything he could associate with water and told him that she would call him shortly to explain the mysterious request and re-direction. Eric was stunned, but he also knew when to swallow his pride and put his ego on hold. He left shortly thereafter. It was then that things got interesting.

The conference center where they were having their meeting had kitchen facilities and Amanda quickly got hold of some straws, eggs, toothpicks, foil, plastic, toilet rolls and a few other sundry supplies. She brought them into the room and asked the group to self-select into two separate teams while distributing the supplies amongst them. Their task, she said, was to build a small raft that could float one member of their team across the stream that was out back of the building. If they could find any more supplies around the building, they were welcome to use them. They had two hours to build it, and they could only communicate with each other through a straw. She advised that this apparently ridiculous exercise was key to kick-starting their creative thinking and asked for their indulgence.

Perhaps it was the needed distraction they welcomed, or maybe it was because they were given no time to reject the exercise, but they were soon devising ways to build their rafts. It wasn't long before the groups were in fits of laughter. During the building, Amanda called Eric to tell him what was happening, explaining that the exercise was a method to improve the emotional tone that would, in turn, boost their creative thinking later. She also told Eric that he was intimidating the others and, in effect, his leadership style was problematic with respect to inspiring the others. He was floored. But for right now, if he would make an effort to refrain from critical comments and just go with the flow, at least for this meeting, she said, then she had a better chance to deliver the results he was looking for. He agreed. The conversation ended with his promise to meet them at the stream to present a prize to the winning team. He was to find some way to reveal the nice guy beneath the surface.

Two hours later they all walked toward the stream, rafts in hand, with each team's hapless victim getting ready to sail. As they approached the water, Eric stepped out from behind a tree wearing a wetsuit, snorkel and mask. It was, as they say, a Kodak moment. If there was ever a way to completely dispel an aura of arrogance, this was it! The sense of humor that was presumed to be non-existent in Eric, was there for all to see. It was a great way to break down the interpersonal barrier that had existed for so long between him and the rest of the group.

The next half hour was taken up with unsuccessful attempts to cross the stream, with both teams getting wet, the 'sailor' of each team getting soaked, and all amidst much laughter. With no clear winner, Eric gave everyone an "Attaperson" award, which was simply a promissory note for a free dinner on behalf of the company. It was a symbolic gesture that went a long way to improving interpersonal relations.

After lunch, and drying off, they were ready to do some brainstorming about the business. Eric made it clear that he would not criticize anyone's ideas and made a point of encouraging comments. Unlike their usual business meetings for this purpose, they forged ahead with some creative thinking techniques generating a large number of interesting ideas. On later follow-up, a new business venture idea that had come up in the earlier session was beginning to show some potential, and Eric confirmed that the culture of the company was changing for the better as he learned to set a better example as a leader.

Leaders need to be aware of the impact they have on others through their emotional self-awareness. It is neither realistic nor desirable to be upbeat and optimistic all of the time, and is simply not the normal human condition. In fact, it isn't possible. We experience the spectrum of emotion from sadness to elation as part of our functioning. We cannot feel happiness unless we have felt sadness. We do not know anxiety unless we have felt calm, and so it goes with every emotion's polarity. Being aware of how you feel helps you recognize your feelings and alter your behavior in a way that does not intimidate or alienate others.

To be sure, fun and games such as these would not be appropriate in many business case scenarios, but when new ideas are sought, they can be very effective. The leader's role in setting the emotional tone for this environment, or at least in not dampening it is, therefore, pivotal.

Psychologists have long known that people will not work to their potential because of extrinsic motivational factors such as money, status or company policies. They might attract employees into the company with these, but what keeps them motivated are intrinsic factors such as praise, responsibility and meaningful work.[13] Employees who feel distressed by stress, critical comments and negativity, generally, do not think clearly and tend to lose interest even when pursuing goals that are important to them.[14] If employees do not feel the freedom to be themselves, it is unlikely that they will be able to give of themselves fully. Employees who are made to feel anxious by bosses that are self-centered, intimidating or blaming, often become preoccupied with the specter of failure and will play it safe. That is, if they stay at all.

In economic cycles when the economy is good and employment is robust, the talented employees who contribute the most to a business don't have to put up with the grief doled out by a bad boss. Your assets walk out the door every night. Providing a secure environment, by bosses who are good listeners, encouraging, optimistic and have a good sense of humor will cause employees to focus better on their work and see obstacles as challenges rather than threats.[15]

If you want to increase the creativity and innovation in your organization, then structure your brainstorming meetings so that there is at least some lightheartedness there. Invite those people who are upbeat and are quick with a joke. You will see how quickly the group's perceptual

---

13   Hertzberg, E. (1968). One More Time: How do you Motivate Employees? *Harvard Business Review,* 46(1) 53-62.
14   Goleman, D. (2006). *Social Intelligence.* New York: Bantam Books.
15   ibid.

lenses open up and find yourself considering possibilities of thinking you normally would not.

Exercise: Using Emotional Intelligence to Work With Employees

Every boss wants to say "no" sometimes. There are ways to say "no" that don't completely shut down the discussion. Try these pairs, and fill in the blanks:

SQUELCH negative	**BETTER positive**
"Not right now."	"See me after."
"You're off topic."	"Great, hold that thought, but let's solve that other problem first."
"Too expensive. It'll never happen."	"How could we pay for that?"
"Where did you get that idea?"	_____
"Too far afield."	_____
"Legal will never go for that."	_____
"They tried that 5 years ago. It won't fly."	_____
"We don't believe in focus groups."	_____
"We can't afford a consultant."	_____

Each one of us wants to be considered intelligent. What better way to do that than to criticize another's ideas in a meeting? It's especially true in a corporate environment in which attendees may be seeking the approval of a boss or a higher-ranking person.

Name three ways in which you have been criticized recently in a meeting.

_____

_____

_____

Now list three ways in which the person doing the criticizing could have been more tactful, and achieved the same goal:

_____

_____

_____

Now name three ways in which you have done something in a meeting that undercut a co-worker in a way that you were not proud of your behavior:

_____

_____

_____

In those incidents: what could you have done better?

_____

Chapter 4

Boundaries are made to be Blurred

There is no better reminder of one's aging than a discussion of computer technology between members of different generations. The other day I called up my software company to find out why something would not work. The conversation went something like this:

Me: "Yes, I'd like some help with adding tables in letters, please."

Rep: "Sure. I can help you with that. What seems to be the problem?"

Me: "Well, every time I go to add in a column, I get this heavy dotted line that goes across the page and I can't delete it. It's very frustrating. I've been at this for nearly an hour."

Rep: "O.K. try this. Place your cursor at the beginning of the line, do a left click on your mouse and drag it across to the end of the line. Then press delete."

Me: "I've tried that and it doesn't work. Nothing happens"

Rep: "All right then. Try this. Highlight the line beginning one line above, and then one below. Press delete."

Me: "I just tried that too, and nothing happens. This is getting frustrating. What else can I do?"

The polite young rep offered about four more suggestions, but nothing seemed to work. I was put on hold a few times in between suggestions, so that he could ask for his supervisor's help. Twenty-five minutes had gone by and my irritation was building. I finally blurted out:

Me: "For crying out loud, I could have gotten this done by now if I just typed it on a typewriter. This is such a time-waster. I can't believe how ridiculous this is!"

Rep: (pausing) "I'm sorry ma'am, but I can't relate."

Me: (*By now I'm ready to scream, what's wrong with this guy? I'm thinking*) "Can't relate?" I repeat, my voice rising. "What do you mean you can't relate?" (*Is this your way of dismissing me because you can't do your job? I think, but refrain from saying.*)

Rep: "I've never seen a typewriter, ma'am."

Me: (*Stunned silence.*)

Rep: "Ma'am? Are you there?"

Me: (*The tone of my voice was much calmer now. Shock had dissipated my anger*) "Yes" I said slowly. "You have NEVER seen a typewriter?"

Rep: "No, ma'am. Never. I've heard about 'em, but never seen one."

How does one spell 'dinosaur'? As a middle-aged woman, it was not the first time I had been reminded of my lost youth, but never before had I felt the stark reality of such a generation gap.

Over the years, like many in my generation, I made the transition from a typewriter to a computer keyboard without thinking much about it, except to enjoy the improvements along the way. The mechanical typewriter was probably the most significant business tool of its' day and was a big time-saver over handwritten methods of communication. The electronic keyboards now are a big improvement enabling the users to fly over the keys with apparent lightening speed. Interestingly, the QWERTY design, which is the set of keys on the left hand top row, have not been changed from its' original design. But is it the best design? When I ask this question of participants in my innovation sessions, they offer post hoc explanations that justify its design. The common assumption is that this design facilitates the letters that are used most often and, therefore, increases our ability to type. A logical answer, but not true. In fact, it is designed to do just the opposite.

The original typewriter, invented by Christopher Latham Sholes in 1868, never imagined that typewriting would be faster than handwriting, which is usually around 20 words per minute or less.[16] The machine was designed in an alphabetical fashion and when a typist pressed a key, a lever would come up with an inked letter and leave the letter's impression on the paper. The problem was that the levers jammed easily so Sholes obtained a list of the most common letters used in English, and reconfigured the keyboard by splitting up those keys to slow down typing. Think about that. The QWERTY design is configured to slow you down. Since most of us use the keyboard as a medium to communicate, our goal is to type as quickly as possible to get the job done. So the next question is: why hasn't someone re-configured the keyboard to increase typing speed?

Well, someone did. It was Sholes. He was even granted a patent on his improved keyboard arrangement in 1896, yet the QWERTY remained the industry standard. Apparently, there was a widespread, albeit erroneous, belief that the benefits of retraining typists were not worth the costs.[17] It's a wonderful example of how assumptions are formed and when they are not questioned, accepted as truths. When something works, why question it? Let it be. As a society, we direct our attention and creativity to those problem areas in an effort to fix them. This is a narrow use of creative thinking and is akin to looking at creativity in the rear view mirror. By focusing on what isn't working, you

---

16   Cassingham, R. C. (1986). *The Dvorak Keyboard*. Arcata, CA.: Freelance Communications.
17   Ibid.

are priming your mind to see only what is there, with an inclination to make small improvements, rather than seeing something totally anew.

Innovators take a more audacious approach, broadening their perspective, and they question the most fundamental aspects of things. Their inherent curiosity dares them to explore new territories of thinking. They question the underlying assumptions and, in effect, get underneath the 'what is'. How do we know what we know? they often ask. For example, how do we know that a fridge is a fridge? We know it because some manufacturer designed an early version of an icebox, which evolved into a refrigerator, whose purpose is to keep things cold. But how did we come to know it as a fridge? asks the innovator. The word refrigerate is a description of its function, no one would argue that, but someone came up with that word for its' description. We've accepted that.

Here is where the audacity comes in. The innovator does not accept that a fridge must be what it has been ordained to be. He blurs the boundary between it and other conveniences offered through other products. He treats the fridge as only a starting point to building something else, and in effect, re-defines the original concept as something totally new, different and a must-have.

Boundaries do not exist for those with an innovative mindset because they know that society, itself, is a human product. Everything in front of us in our society is the product of someone's thinking and it is all up for challenging and changing.

In challenging the fridge, the innovator asks: Why can't the fridge have other functions, refusing to accept that it can only keep things cold. Now the fun begins. He suggests that a fridge should be able to heat things up, prepare the food and serve meals. "But then it isn't a fridge." objects the market taker. "Precisely." says the innovator, and as if having taken up the gauntlet, continues "it should have an automatic inventory control mechanism that contacts the local grocery store when supplies need replacement so that you never have to go to the grocery store again."

The groceries will be delivered to your door. You won't have to worry about groceries spoiling on your doorstep, either, because the innovator's fridge comes in separate pieces that look nothing like a fridge. One piece of the fridge is embedded into the side of your house where the delivery guy just has to open up the small door, hook up the moving belt from the truck to your fridge entrée ramp, press go and your groceries are sent into the house to the cooler. The frozen foods are packaged in recyclable containers that keep the contents frozen. When they are emptied, the containers are picked up by that same delivery guy the next week, and the process begins again. The fridge is no longer that boxy unit that sits in the kitchen. It is in modular formats found throughout your house for convenience.

The modular format means that you can have a small module in the family room where you can access only drinks and snacks. It can serve as a microwave, too, to heat up those snacks as you view your large screen TV. The larger module will be in the kitchen where you need your cooking supplies. For the weight conscious, you can attach some sort of scale to remind you of your weight and some advice as to whether you should be eating that snack. That could be enough to stoke the guilt and add a weight watcher function to this! A nutritional readout of each snack will accompany your choice.

Clearly, the fridge is now more than a fridge. It is a multi-functional unit that adds convenience to the whole domestic food experience. The innovator has only begun. Adding even more conveniences, this fridge can have a screensaver on the front that shows your favorite photos, provide access to your emails, contain software that enables you to write letters, organize your calendar, design a website, make a video and play music. He is limited only by his imagination.

Now refrigeration is only a small part of what it does. The innovator has cut across the boundaries of one product and into many others because he knows that boundaries are socially constructed. By the time he finishes with his re-design of the fridge, it will be something totally different and unrecognizable, and he will have to name it something else that more closely fits its many functions. Let's call it a "Convenience Unit" for now. If he does his job well, his grandchildren will one day say in a history class: "Can you believe that people had fridges in their homes? And all those cumbersome gadgets? How did they keep track of all of that? It must have been a lot of work."

This is the difference between a market maker rather than a market taker. This innovator has not only designed a product for the market, as the market maker, but defined what it is to a broader market so that the market taker accepts that definition. It now has set a new standard against which everything else in its class is compared.

You might be thinking that a dose of reality is overdue right now because you've just read the musings of someone with a long wish list about a mundane product. Your logic may tell you this is silly as only a few of these ideas could actually work. But here is where you make the effort to stop the voice of judgment and force yourself to see the seeds of ideas. You are diverging to dream for the ultimate conveniences and you must now maintain that open-mindedness to consider the possibilities before you converge back to reality. The further out you go, the more seeds of ideas you will see, and that will increase the number of workable ideas you can finally get. You will find that your reality will grow to include what was once considered not possible.

Once a long list of attributes are generated for the new and improved product, choosing ones to actually add requires a re-combination of them to form a new design. Ever cognizant of the power of questions, the innovator avoids binary questions such as "Can we turn the fridge into an oven too?" which asks for a yes or no answer. The innovator instead asks "How can we add heating capabilities?" with the purposeful assumption that it will be done.

There is never an implication in an innovator's questions whether something is possible. In the mindset of an innovator, there is always a possibility waiting to be discovered. As he goes down the list of alternatives, it becomes evident that incorporating many of them is doable. Automatic inventory control, nutritional counts, and various computer features are all in existence today in some form or another, and that means that the innovator can borrow those examples and now begin to add them. Perhaps they cannot be added in their totality, but they can in pieces. For instance, a computer monitor and LCD screen can be attached to many things, so why not to the front of a modularized Convenience Unit? You can add the nutritional counts of your favorite foods in a databank in your computer and then pull it up on the screen every time you reach for that food. Automatic inventory control might seem like a stretch, but it's not that far away.

The advent of the bar code technology has made inventory tracking possible. Almost every item purchased from a grocery store, department store, and mass retailer has a barcode on it. In fact, researchers have even placed tiny barcodes on individual bees to track the insects' mating habits.[18] So it isn't unlikely that one day your fridge will have a scanner too. Until then, we don't have to stop here simply because we don't have

---

18   Barcode. 30 Retrieved Dec. 2008. from http://en.wikipedia.org/wiki/Barcode.

a scanner. Take a piece of the scanner idea and ask what you can do. You can program your computer calendaring system to remind you of the weekly or monthly food items you like to have on hand. You can see it on the LCD panel on your Convenience Unit, which has automatically sent you the reminder on your handheld if you want to stop at the store on the way home. At least you won't forget them anymore.

Blurring the boundaries between products is a method of innovating that forces you to see past limitations that have been imposed by others' thinking. Remember that a fridge is only a fridge because someone said it was. That was their limit, not yours. The iPhone is a modern example that blurs boundaries between products by converging multiple products into one. It is a cell phone with a calendar, telephone, a portable media player, a camera, a text messaging service with access to Internet facilities such as web browsing, local Wi-Fi connectivity, e-mail and GPS.

Less technical, but no less innovative, is the boundary-blurring product of temperature-adjusted clothing.[19] We have come a long way from wearing too many layers of clothing and women wearing corsets too tight that damaged their internal organs. But the innovator looks forward and asks why we cannot do better. Why should we have to bother putting on a coat at all when we go from a warm temperature to a cold one? she asks, and an idea is spawned by refusing to accept the conventional thinking on clothing. A patent is now pending on clothing that adjusts its temperature to climate conditions.

The aptly named Octopus card is another great example of reaching across boundaries to add convenience and simplicity. You'll find it in Hong Kong, Shenzhen and Macau. The Cantonese name for it is *Baat Daaht Tūng* which means reading everywhere. As a rechargeable smart

---

19 *Body temperature-adjustable clothing.* Retrieved February 28, 2009 from http://www. freepatentsonline.com/EP1329167.html.

card, it is similar to a credit card that can be used for a host of things. It began as a card for not only all public transport in Hong Kong, but now is used for payment at convenience stores, super-markets, fast-food restaurants, on-street parking meters, car parks, and other point-of-sale applications such as service stations and vending machines. Just think of how much thinner your wallet would be if you could carry only one card?

Adopting an audacious attitude means appreciating that everything you see around you in the form of products and services is the thinking of someone else before you. You have the choice to accept them, change them, or re-define them entirely. Embracing this attitude is freeing in the mind and that liberty is the foundation for forming an innovator's mindset.

Exercise: Blurring the Boundaries

Practice blurring the boundaries between products by merging different products together to see what new products you can come up with:

Example: Add a teacup, teabag, saucer, warmer and cookies together. You can get a teacup with a compartment at the side of the cup to hold the teabag out of sight, that sits on top of a battery operated warming saucer with an attached shelf underneath that to hold a few cookies. It is an all-in-one tea-time snack.

Let's try another one. Add a coffee table, a light, coasters, a TV remote control and TV. What can you come up with? You can get a new design for a coffee table whose surface is an LCD screen with a touchpad to replace the remote control. This screen can be folded up perpendicular to the table for viewing. Adding distance between you and the screen now requires a remote control so you would have that sitting in a recessed shelf underneath the table, akin to the shelves that hold computer keyboards, that also holds books and magazines. Coasters can be built into the surface of the table hidden by covers made of the table surface material, to be opened when needed.

The goal of this is to play with the ideas and see what you come up with. Let your mind wander. What can you do by blending these together?

A clock + bedroom night table + a phone + message pad + calendar?

_____

A jacket + car keys + sunglasses + water bottle + cell phone?

_____

A desk + computer + PDA + pens + coffee percolator?

_____

Chapter 5

Borrowing Mother Nature's Innovations

"Study nature. Love nature. Stay close to nature.
It will never fail you."

Frank Lloyd Wright

Before the 2010 BP oil spill in the Gulf of Mexico, the Exxon Valdez spill in 1989 had been considered one of the most devastating environmental disasters ever to have occurred. Thousands of miles of ocean were also covered in oil. In both of these instances, the television coverage that followed showed many heartbreaking pictures of otters, birds and various wildlife species caught in the sludge trying in vain to escape their fate. In the Exxon Valdez television coverage one viewer, an Alabama hairdresser, Phillip McCrory, noticed that volunteers had particular difficulty in cleaning the oil from the otter's fur, as it seemed to soak up the oil well. He wondered, if animal's fur can trap and hold spilled oil, then why can't human hair?"

He subsequently made a pair of tights, stuffed it with hair swept from his salon floor and dumped it into his son's wading pool where he had dumped a gallon of used motor oil. In minutes the water was clear. He had found a solution for cleaning up oil and not only that, but he found that the solution itself had another unexpected benefit. The hair adsorbed, rather than absorbed, the oil so that instead of bonding with the hair, the oil gathered in layers on the hair's surface making it easier to recover and reuse by simply squeezing it from the hair bundles.

Some clients of his who worked at NASA put him in touch with technology transfer agent who did a large scale test. It was discovered that 1.4 million pounds of hair in re-usable mesh pillows could have soaked up the entire 11 million gallons spilled by the Exxon Valdez in about a week. Ironically, Exxon had spent $2 billion on a lengthy cleanup that captured only about 12 per cent of the spill.[20]

If McCrory hadn't been a hairdresser, it is unlikely that he would have come up with this idea. We all see the same things in front of us, but what we pay attention to is determined by our life experiences and all of those things that make us who we are. In fact, according to the Swiss psychologist, Carl Jung, we are neurologically wired to see what we see. Some of us are better at noticing the details, others the big picture. Regardless of our propensity one way or the other though, a skill of creative thinking is to become more aware of what is in front of us. If we could take off our perceptual filters and see from a position of neutrality, without any preconceptions or assumptions, the visual spectrum would expand and we'd notice more.

Amazingly, there are examples of innovation right in front of us that have largely gone unnoticed. Biomimicry (from bios, meaning life, and mimesis, meaning to imitate) is a new science that studies nature's best ideas and then imitates these designs and processes to solve human problems. Its' premise is that nature is imaginative by necessity and has already solved many of the problems we are grappling with. Plants, animals and microbes, in their evolution over the last 3.8 billions years, have effectively been conducting research and development, discovering what works and what doesn't. In nature, there is no pollution or waste, and everything is recycled. Biologists, architects and engineers are now

---

20 At the time of this writing there is much controversy regarding the methods that BP is using to clean up its spill. Surface skimming, burning and spraying dispersants are apparently their main approaches with little or no mention of natural scientific methods.

coming together to find and catalog these biological systems in order to emulate them for innovation.

One example is the lotus plant in Asia. Scientists noticed that its' leaves remain clean and dry despite the fact that it grows in muddy and often polluted swamps. To the naked eye the leaves appear to be smooth, but under a microscope, they are quite mountainous. When it rains, droplets of moisture, coagulate in the leaf valleys and as water levels rise, droplets roll off, carrying the dirt particles with them. Known as the Lotus Effect, this led to the development of a product called Lotusan®, a building façade paint with the lotus effect, marketed by Sto AG Lotusan. Allowing rainwater to do the exterior natural cleaning of buildings is now saving companies thousands of dollars in time, energy and human resources.

Researchers at GE have now applied this concept to plastic that is naturally hydrophilic (water-attracting) and to metals used in industrial products. The goal is to increase the efficiency of wind and gas turbine blades and fan blades of jet engines by effectively de-icing them with this technology.[21] Carrying this concept further, researchers are looking at ways to apply the lotus effect to bathroom mirrors, automobile paints, roof shingles and even clothing. Its' application will surely be broadened from here, too, as surfaces treated with it have ninety percent fewer germs than surfaces coated with conventional paints opening up the medical arena for more applications.

Self-cleaning surfaces have another use in nature when it comes to moving through water. The shark is one example of a species whose hydrodynamic, and other, properties are providing inspiration to boat builders and swim suit makers. Seawater has countless ecto-parasites

---

21   Schlett, J. (2008, November 30). Blossoming technology: GE scientists imitate lotus plant, nano-treat metals to repel water. *Daily Gazette.*

(algae, bacteria and barnacle larvae) within it that hinder the movement through it, yet sharks are able to move through it efficiently. The reason is that their skin, despite its' smooth appearance, similar to the lotus leaf, has many small individual ribbed scales called dermal denticles ("little skin teeth").

These dermal scales continually flex in response to changes in internal and external pressure associated with the shark's movement reducing the available surface area for adherence. They also serve to reinforce the direction of water flow by accelerating it at the skin's surface reducing the contact time of the ecto-parasites. All of this reduces the friction drag, which is of great interest to boat manufacturers because organisms attaching to a ship's hull are major sources of energy inefficiency.[22] Surface coatings inspired by shark skin have shown a 67% decrease in organism attachments and are completely self-cleaning at 4-5 knots.[23]

The swimsuit company, Speedo, has designed the Fastskin swimsuit, with this technology incorporated into their swimsuits. This suit has resulted in a 3% improvement in swimming speed. Perhaps it is no coincidence that 80% of the swimming medals won in the 2000 Olympics were won by athletes wearing these suits and that those swimmers also broke 13 of 15 world records.[24]

UltraCane® is another successful example of a nature inspired innovation taken from the bat. Bats have very poor eyesight yet can navigate accurately in the darkness through the process of echolocation. They send out sound waves using their mouth or nose and when the sound hits an object, an echo comes back letting them know how far away they are from it. UltraCane® is an electronic mobility aid that uses

---

22 *Biomimicking Sharks*. Retrieved December 29, 2008 from http://www.biomimicry institute
    .org/home-page-content/home-page-content/biomimicking-sharks.html
23 ibid.
24 ibid.

ultrasonic signals that bounce off objects in the environment, alerting the user to obstacles in the way.

It is astounding to imagine the sheer number and diversity of innovative solutions found in nature and to think that we've only just begun to find them. As a source of innovation, it is both wondrous and maddening because it is marked by its simplicity and complexity. We need only to look at nature right there in front of us, yet how it evolved that way and the mechanisms that explain its' success, often eludes us. We look, but cannot always see, particularly when the solutions appear so counterintuitive. But we will keep trying to crack the code of this vast treasure chest of innovation, as did the engineers in the example of the Australian Boxfish.

DaimlerChrysler, it turns out, has introduced the diesel-powered "Bionic Concept Vehicle," fashioned after this very un-aerodynamic fish.[25] This species have large spikes and horns protruding from their skin and unlike most fish, uses its pectoral fins to cruise through the water. Its' tail fin is used only for acceleration when it needs to escape a predator, for example. As we learn more about this fish, we realize that it doesn't need aerodynamic (or more accurately, hydrodynamic) properties because it is a slow-moving fish built for safety, not for speed.

If you were exploring ways to improve the aerodynamic properties of the airplane wing, you probably wouldn't look at the boxfish because, like it or not, the law of physics just wouldn't allow you to design a wing for an airplane to be slow-moving. You probably wouldn't look toward the humpback whale either, but this time, you would be overlooking a source of innovation inspiration.

---

25 *Mercedes-Benz Bionic Concept Vehicle: Examining The Great Potential of Bionics*, 2005. Retrieved December 29, 2008 from http://www.world.carfans.com/2050607 .005

The scalloped flipper of the humpback whale is a superior design, as two scientists, James D. Watt of the Cornell Laboratory of Ornithology and Frank Fish, a professor of biology at West Chester University in Pennsylvania, discovered. [26] The two found that these scalloped flippers not only have a more efficient wing design than the smooth edges used on airplanes, but also have one-third less drag and better lift properties, and they withstood stall at a 40 percent steeper wind angle. Further, this design is useful not just for airplane wings, but also for helicopter rotor tips, propellers and ship rudders. The benefits include a greater margin of safety, improved plane maneuverability, and better fuel efficiency, lowering one of the major cost factors in flying.

If you worked in the field of aerodynamics, but you weren't an ichthyologist, it is unlikely that you would have found these sources of innovation. So, the innovator asks, where might you look in nature for some ideas?

Jay Harman, of Pax Scientific, found his inspiration in an extraordinarily common thing, from which he took his blueprint for industrial design. It was water.[27]

As a boy, Harman noticed that fluids and gases flow not in straight lines, but rather in spirals. Years later, after watching the water flow down the drain out of his bathtub, he designed a cast from the vortex created by the flow. He then used the cast to help redesign the rotating parts, or impellers, used in pumps and other devices to move fluids more efficiently and with less noise. Capitalizing on that design, Harman is now designing quieter and more energy-efficient fans for the computer industry.

---

26 Benyus, J. (2002). *Biomimicry: Innovation Inspired by Nature*. New York: William Morrow & Co.

27 Markoff, J. (2008, June 8). Nature Gave Him a Blueprint, but not Overnight Success. *New York Times.*

Nature has a lot to teach us about movement in general. The kingfisher's beak was used as inspiration for the design of the nose on the bullet train in Japan. With the strictest noise standards for rail operation in the world, engineers in Japan had to find a way to reduce the sonic boom that occurred upon exiting tunnels.[28] The long beak allows this bird to absorb sudden changes in air pressure as it dives into water to hunt food. Mimicking this design eliminated the problem.

Engineers also replicated the serration feathers found on an owl's wings that allow them to fly stealthily through the night. They are small saw-toothed feathers that protrude from the outer rim of their primary feathers. Apparently, they generate small vortexes in the air flow that break up the larger vortexes, which produce noise. The engineers incorporated the serration design into the devices that connect the trains to the overhead electrical wires, significantly reducing noise once again.

Biomimicry is extraordinary not only because it is an incredible source of innovation. Perhaps the largest benefit of this discipline is that all of its innovations are life-enhancing and additive, not destructive or degrading to the world in which we live. The solutions in nature do not compromise our environment in the form of waste or pollution, unlike our own man-made endeavors.

Turning limestone into structural material is a good example. E. Robertson[29] of the Biomass Institute in Winnipeg, Canada, points out, man has found three ways that we do this: Cut it into blocks, grind it up, and then heat it up to 2,700 degrees F to turn it into cement, using

---

28 Japan for Sustainability Newsletter,(2005) # 031. *Biomimicry Interview Series No. 6. Technologies Learned from Living Things: Concepts and Examples – Front Line Reports.* Shinkansen Technology Learned from an Owl: The Story of Eiji Nakatsu. Retrieved December 29, 2008 from http://www.japanfs.org/en/newsletter/200303-2.html
29 Benyus, J. ibid.

lots of energy in the heating process. In fact, for every ton of cement manufactured, a ton of carbon dioxide is emitted into the atmosphere.[30] Carbon dioxide is a significant contributor to greenhouse gases and, therefore, global warming.

Mother Nature, on the other hand, has a simpler way: simply feed it to a chicken and get it back hours later as an even stronger eggshell. And if we were as smart as clams and oysters, he says, we might turn the limestone into structural material slowly at 40 degrees F. Of course, in nature, where diversity reigns, we do not have to rely on feeding chickens to produce sturdy structural materials.

The abalone shell has alternating layers of calcium carbonate that end up with an architectural template to build a shell that is twice as tough as any high-tech ceramic. And let's not forget the lowly spider, whose web rivals the strength of high-grade steel, and is as strong as Kevlar. The spider silk is extremely lightweight. If there were a strand of spider silk long enough that it could encircle the earth, it would weigh less than 16 ounces.[31] Less effort, no waste and no pollution.

Anyone observing nature may find it hard to comprehend the beautiful hues it displays. They will always serve as an inspiration to the artists who try to capture them on canvas. And here, again, nature's superiority over ours in producing color is remarkable. We use paint, with pigments that are often toxic, and the painted surfaces must be re-painted over time as they degrade. Then we have the responsibility of disposing of leftover paint and paint cans, which are quite damaging to the environment. How, then, does nature supply color without harm or waste?

---

30 Hawken, P., Lovins, A. and Hunter-Lovins, I. (1999). *Natural Capitalism: Creating the Next Industrial Revolution.* New York: Little Brown & Company.
31 Spider Silk. Retrieved November 11, 2008 from http://www.en.wikipedia.org/wiki/Spider_silk.

Look no further than the feathers, scales and skeletons of iridescent birds, butterflies and beetles for one answer. Nothing is added to supply color; rather, the color is structural, because the features of the scales and feathers cause light to diffract and interfere in ways that amplify certain wavelengths, resulting in color that is four times brighter than pigment. The scales and feathers never need repainting and there are no toxic effects with the pigments. Disposal is a non-issue.

Teijin Fibers Limited, a Japanese company, was one of the first companies to capitalize on this natural strategy with a product called Morphotex®, inspired by the Morpho butterfly. It is a pigment-free fiber that produces vibrant self-illuminating color using a light interference strategy right in the fabric itself.

A U.S. company, Qualcomm, used the same idea, but in a different way. They developed the Interferometric Modulator (IMOD), a micro-electro-mechanical system device that is composed of two conductive plates.[32] One is a thin film stack on a glass substrate medium, the other is a reflective membrane suspended over the substrate medium with a gap between the two that is filled with air. The plates are separated when no voltage is applied, allowing the light hitting the substrate to be reflected. When a small voltage is applied, the plates are pulled together by electrostatic attraction and the light is absorbed, turning the element black. The result is a low-energy screen that you can read in the sunlight.

With a little innovation paint doesn't have to be damaging to the environment. Take, for example, StoClimasan Color. It is an interior paint manufactured by a company called Sto in Germany, without the detrimental effects. In fact, this product actually purifies air by breaking down odors and other airborne pollutants when exposed to artificial

---

32 *Mirasol Displays: A Qualcomm Innovation Inspired by Nature.* Retrieved 2008, July 03 from http://www.qualcomm_products_services/consumer_electronics/ displays/mirasol/index.html

light.[33] It works on the principle of photosynthesis in nature. Green leaves convert energy into chemical energy to produce sugar, and release oxygen into the atmosphere. The actual blueprint for the innovation is based on the chlorophyll in the leaves that traps the ultraviolet light energy required to trigger the transformation.

A similar innovation exists in the world of building materials. An Italian company, the Italcementi Group, has designed a concrete, called TX Active, that essentially cleans itself, minimizing the need for maintenance.[34] The mechanism to make this happen is the titanium dioxide that "eats" surrounding smog. When it is exposed to sunlight, the titanium dioxide is activated and pollutants that come in contact with the cement surface are oxidized. Hazardous nitrogen oxides and sulfur oxides are transformed into harmless nitrates or sulfates, which then rinse off the building with rainwater.

Apparently, extensive testing, sponsored in part by a European Union research project into "smart" antipollution materials, has determined that construction products containing titanium dioxide help to destroy other air pollutants found in car exhaust and heating emissions. Several companies are developing "smog-eating" products that can be used in paint, plaster and paving materials for roads. These are environmentally friendly substances that are being tried out in buildings and highways in Europe as well as Japan.

There is no doubt that these sorts of innovations are admirable as well as much needed in cleaning up the pollution we have inflicted on the environment. What is striking about the innovations inspired by nature, as compared to others, is that the natural ones are less labor-intensive and use

---

33 No More Smells. *Sto News*. Retrieved July 03, 2008 from http://www.sto.co.uk/evo/web/ sto/26514_EN-News Details.
34 *Provoledo, E. Architecture in Italy Goes Green*. 2006. International Herald Tribune: Europe. Retrieved October12, 2008 from http://www.iht.com/articles/2006/11/22 news/smog.php.

existing materials rather than manufacturing new ones. Temperature control is a good example.

We use oil, electricity or other fossil fuels to heat our homes and buildings in the winter, and to cool them in the summer. But fossil fuels are costly and degrade the environment. While the invention of solar panels leads us in the right direction for using nature's bounty of sunlight, there are other possibilities.

Consider this example of everyday materials used in a sophisticated way by termites in Zimbabwe. They live in tall mounds of dried mud, where they farm a fungus as their primary source of food. This fungus must be kept at exactly 87 degrees Fahrenheit, and the termites maintain this temperature inside while outside the temperature ranges from 35 degrees Fahrenheit at night to 104 degrees Fahrenheit during the day. To achieve this laudable feat, the termites constantly open and close a series of heating and cooling vents throughout the mound in the day. The air is sucked in at the lower part of the mound and then up through a channel to the peak of the mound, in a system of carefully adjusted convection currents.

Engineers have mimicked this design in two buildings that form a mid-rise office and shopping center in Harare, Zimbabwe, where the temperature is regulated year-round without any air-conditioning or heating.[35] Air is continuously drawn from an open space between the two buildings and pushed up vertically through ducts located in the central spine of each building. The fresh air replaces stale air that rises and exists through exhaust ports in the ceilings. The complex uses less than 10 percent of the energy of a conventional building its size; the owners estimate that they will reap a savings of $3.5 million in air-conditioning costs alone.

---

35 Doan, Abigail. (2007). Green Building in Zimbabwe Modeled After Termite Mounds. 2007. *Inhabitat*. Retrieved October 12, 2008 from http://www.inhabitat.com /2007/12/10/ building-modelled-on-termites-eastgate-centre-in- Zimbabwe.

Tenants save, too, with rents 20 percent lower than those of occupants in surrounding buildings. Who would ever guess that termites could show us how to design an eco-friendly structure with climate control and cost-effectiveness too?

The mere thought of termites might send a homeowner over the edge, but there is another less bug-centric option to cut costs in climate control. Simply put a garden on the roof. Green roofs bring aesthetic appeal, but not only that: they also have numerous other benefits.[36] A roof that has been specially prepared to carry soil or vermiculite or a mix can be planted with ground covers or other plants that will last up to twice as long as conventional roofs, reduce storm water runoff, improve air quality and result in significant savings in energy heating and cooling costs. Beyond that, a garden insulates for sound. Sound waves that are produced by machinery, traffic or airplanes can be absorbed, reflected or deflected. A green roof with 4.7 inches of substrate layer can reduce sound by 40 decibels; 7.9 inches of substrate layer can reduce sound by 46-50 decibels. As the world becomes more populated, this becomes a more important consideration.

There is a green alternative to the pink fiberglass insulation homeowners have used for decades in the colder climates, and it doesn't get any greener. Greensulate is the name of an insulation made by Ecovative Design in Troy, N.Y. It is made from water, oyster mushroom fibers, rice hulls and recycled paper that resists temperature change, repels water and retards fire.[37] It is less costly than traditional insulation because the rice hulls are considered agricultural garbage, and a panel of any size

---

36 *About Green Roofs* Retrieved April 9, 2008 from http//www.greenroofs.org/ index.
    php?option=com.
37 Bosch, A. (2008) Staying Cool: Green Insulation Gets Warm Reception. *Scientific American,*
    28

can be grown within one to two weeks. No complicated manufacturing process is needed. Just a place that is big and dark to grow it.

As we have seen, sometimes the sources for innovation in nature are not the most obvious choices for observation and inspiration. Remember the temperature-adjusted clothing idea that was spawned by notion of blurring boundaries? Well, once again nature has already solved that in the nondescript pinecone.

Julian Vincent, professor of biomimetics at the University of Bath in the United Kingdom, found that pinecones have two layers of stiff fibers running in different directions to open up and release their seeds when they fall to the ground.[38] The seed release is stimulated by the lack of water as the pinecones are cut off from the tree. Using this example, Vincent and his team designed a "breathing" fabric to stop the wearer getting hot or cold by adjusting itself to both internal and external temperatures. The textile is made of a layer of thin spikes of water-absorbent material that stand up, perpendicular to the surface, when made wet by the wearer's sweat. When the layer dries out, the spikes automatically lie down parallel to the surface. A second layer underneath protects the wearer from the rain.

This is more than a mere convenience to the average consumer. For starters, this type of adaptive "smart fabric" would be valuable to the defense industry because fewer layers of clothing need to be worn, especially in areas of the world with widely fluctuating temperatures. A soldier in the desert in the Middle East, for instance, would need only a few layers during the day in the baking heat, but lots of layers at night when the temperature drops significantly.

---

38 *New Smart-Fabric Inspired by Pine Cones* Retrieved May 28, 2008 from http://www. gizmag. com/go/3515

An interesting and innovative clothing project that is not strictly a biomimetic innovation is a jacket grown from living tissue developed by the Australian-based Tissue Culture and Art Project.[39] This garment is grown from a combination of mouse and human cells; it was created in an attempt to produce "victimless leather." For those concerned about the lives of the mice, there is consolation in the fact that cell lines produced from the actual cells are far greater in number than the actual number of cells. Tons or even tens of tons can come from one mouse.[40] If nothing else, these semi-living products will raise a few questions as well as a few eyebrows.

Another case of a natural and unexpected inspiration is the lowly ant. As it turns out, the company American Air Liquide found that ants have things to teach us. The company makes industrial and medical gases, mostly nitrogen, oxygen and hydrogen, at about 100 locations in the United States and delivers these gases to 6,000 sites via railcars, pipelines and 400 trucks. As if that isn't enough to look after, the company encounters price pressures as a result of deregulated power markets where electricity prices can change every 15 minutes.

Working with NuTech Solutions, a firm that specializes in artificial intelligence, Air Liquide developed a computer model to seek out good, inexpensive transport routes based on algorithms inspired by Argentine ants.

When ants forage for food, they come back to the nest leaving a trail of pheromones that other ants can sense by smell, telling other ants to go get more food. Every time an ant goes out, it reinforces the trail. The computer program was developed to send out billions of messages,

---

39 *Victimless Leather: A Prototype of Stitch-less Jacket Grown in a Technoscientific Body.* Retrieved February 11, 2009 from http://www.tca.uwa.edu.au/vl/vl/html
40 Lakshmi, S. (2004) Jacket Grows from Living Tissue. *Wired.* Retrieved February 13, 2009 from http://www.wired.com/science/discoveries/news/2004/10/65248

something akin to software "ants", to find out where the trails are strongest for their truck routes.

Air Liquide combined this approach with other artificial techniques to consider various aspects of plant scheduling, truck routing and other logistical issues, together with customer demand forecasts and manufacturing costs. Every morning the company's managers have computer-generated advice as to where the shipment pickups would reap the greatest savings.

As this example shows us, it doesn't matter if an idea is used literally or metaphorically, so long as the idea leads to an innovation. Southwest Airlines also used this idea metaphorically by developing an ant-based computer model to decrease waiting on the runway for its planes. Rather than leaving virtual pheromones along the way, each plane learned how to reduce wait time on the tarmac by "remembering" the faster gates and "forgetting" the slower ones with the help of real data fed into the computer model.

Learning from Mother Nature requires that we first look with a cultivated sense of curiosity and focus our sights on what we see, not what we *think* we see, as if we are noticing what is in front of us for the first time. That helps us step back and question the most fundamental attributes. Ask questions such as "Why did this evolve this way? What purposes does it serve?" Or frame the questions to a problem that needs a resolution.

Boeing did this by recently sending some engineers to Costa Rica[41] to find out ways to reduce the noise inside a plane's cabin. A plane's walls hold fiberglass blankets that insulate passengers from noise and the cold outside, but weight restrictions preclude adding more of them. This

---

41   Harmon, P. Biomimicry conference in La Cusinga Lodge, Costa Rica. April, 2008

problem is further complicated by the fact that eliminating too much noise would mean passengers would hear each other's every cough.

So the question the engineers asked was this: What creature's survival depends on managing noise or vibration? Apparently, cicadas, leaf cutter ants and some birds actively shape the noise they make, offering up some ideas with great potential. The leaf cutter ant, for example, produces high-frequency vibrations through its mandibles to stiffen the leaves it cuts. Translating this concept of shaping noise opens up new directions of thinking for the Boeing engineers.

I walked through a rain forest with these engineers, and it didn't take long to find more inspiration for innovation in the spider. In many a tree, spiders sat in their large webs with the sunlight shining through. So long as you were not an arachnophobic, it was a pretty sight. Their web design was particularly intriguing because they apparently weave strands in different levels of thicknesses to achieve flexibility and strength.

To catch a flying insect, the spider's web must absorb the kinetic energy to slow its motion to a halt. The force required to stop the insect's motion is inversely proportional to the distance over which the motion must be stopped.[42] The longer the distance over which the insect can be slowed down, the smaller the force necessary to stop it, and the less potential for damage to the web. Of more interest to the engineers, of course, is the fact that the insects caught in the web cause vibrations that alert the spider to the location of its next meal. If the engineers could determine where vibrations occur most in the plane, they mused, then perhaps they could design a structure to dampen that noise.

---

42   Kennedy, S. (2007). Biomimicry/Biomimetics: General Principles and Practical Examples. *The Science Creative Quarterly, 3.*

This is exactly the sort of thinking that biomimicry stokes in the innovator's mind. As an avenue for creativity and innovation, using biomimicry means looking at an area of nature that achieves what you are trying to do. Here are a few more examples of man-made innovations to get you thinking:

- The mechanism allowing the submarine's ascent and descent was designed after the principle of a fish bladder, which inflates or deflates with gas to change depth

- The mechanism of a camera's automatic focus came from the principles of the human eye's functions

- The design of the hypodermic needle is based on the way venomous snakes deliver poison through their fangs

Exercise: Using Biomimicry to Innovate

Take heart that you don't need a Ph.D. in biology to use biomimicry as your source of innovation. Access to information, such as that on the Internet, will give you a good start. If you are looking for answers to design dilemmas, follow this type of question template, with the following biomimicry example:

Design Dilemma: Keeping a building cool without air conditioning (as another alternative to the termite construction. In nature, remember that diversity reigns. There are usually multiple ways to achieve the same effect).

Questions to Ask:

1. What natural environments have similar conditions to those in which my dilemma exists?

Answer: Deserts have plenty of heat.

2. What creatures live in those environments?

Answer: Cacti, among other things.

3. Research those creatures. What do you notice about their structure?

Answer: Cacti are often tall and have vertical 'ribs' or folds with sharp thistles on it.

4. How does this structure enable it to survive?

Answer: The vertical ribs shade the cactus against the sun. This shape creates alternating areas of shade and light along the ribs which, in turn, produces rising and falling air currents that improve heat radiation. And when the sun reaches its highest position, it hits the cactus from above, where the least amount of its surface appears.

5. What ideas can you take away to replicate their design?

Answer: Build the outer layer of a building using the rib design.

Don't be concerned if you cannot find your answers right away. Study the element in nature and ask what purpose its' design serves. The answer may not be immediately obvious. It may not even be known just yet. There is still so much that we don't know about the environment in which we live, but engineers, scientists and architects are adding to this fascinating body of knowledge every day.[43] And you might too.

---

43 See www.AskNature.org of the Biomimicry Guild for their up to date databank of innovation examples

Chapter 6

Changing Climate and Natural Selection - Biomimicry to the Rescue

A significant issue looming in front of all of us, and one that frames many questions, is that of global warming. It is ironic that the damage we are inflicting upon nature – damage that contributes to global warming – can sometimes be un-done by mimicking that which we destroy. In essence, we are killing our teachers.

Nature continues to surprise us with the sheer diversity of strategies it uses to survive, and we benefit greatly from that diversity because of the number of ideas we can borrow from it.

Take, for example, the issue of changing water levels around the world, as one aspect of the global warming crisis. Not only are we witnessing more floods than ever before in some areas, but in other areas we are also experiencing debilitating droughts.

That simply observed fact raises a number of questions. How does nature accommodate changing water levels? What in nature can live in floods as well as droughts? How does nature provide protection from the elements?

Nature shows us plenty of examples. Wetlands are a natural place to look for ideas, because they constantly experience fluctuations in water levels. In fact, wetlands have a variety of water depths where plants that are normally submersed may have to endure periods without any water at all.

And yet they survive, by means of a mechanism called phenotypic plasticity, or the ability to change their morphology. They can, quite simply, adjust their growth as water levels change.

In building structures close to the water's edge, an immediate danger is a building that will block water, and therefore become vulnerable to its pressure. If you look at plants that grow in water, you will often see long, narrow, relatively sturdy stems, which allow water to flow through them. We can take this idea and build homes on stilts to avoid obstructing water flows.

The concept of going with the water was embraced by the French architect, Vincent Callebaut, who used the water lily as an inspiration when he designed a completely self-sufficient floating city intended to provide shelter for refugees from future climate change.[44] Called the Lilypad, it is intended to be a zero emission city afloat in the ocean. Using technologies including solar, wind, tidal and biomass, this project he envisioned would be able to not only produce its own energy, but also to process carbon dioxide in the atmosphere and absorb it into the structure's titanium dioxide skin.

Each floating Lilypad is designed to hold around 50,000 people. The landscape is a mixed terrain that includes an artificial lagoon and three ridges, creating a diverse environment for the inhabitants. Each Lilypad, according to his concept, would be either near a coast, or floating in the ocean, traveling from the equator to the northern seas, according to where the Gulf Stream takes it.

On a smaller scale, the daddy longlegs spider has some lessons for us in accommodating to changing water levels. These insects have legs

---

44   Chapa, J. (2008). *Lilypad: Floating City for Climate Change Refugees."* Retrieved
     January 9, 2009 from http://www.inhabitat.com/2008/06/16/lilypad-floating-cities-i-the-
     age-of-globalwarming/#more -11777.

that have muscles to flex the joints, but none to extend them.[45] To extend those legs, they have developed an effective hydraulic mechanism: When a spider gets ready to jump, for a fraction of a second, it generates excess pressure in its legs, and then the legs extend to accommodate more fluid. From here it is not that much of a jump to design the underside of buildings with similar mechanisms for vertical movement to accommodate changing water levels.

Mangroves are another wonderful example of survival in changing water levels, as well as water desalination, which is an important issue because most of the Earth's cover is salt water. Basically, mangroves extract salt from water via transpiration and filtering through their membranes, and they do all of this in a harsh environment.

Twice a day the tide rises to cover their roots, and then recedes to expose those roots to the air. Moreover, that water changes: it is salty in the tide's rise, but nearly fresh with the tide's flow out to sea. The slightest eddy in the current will remove the mud that was deposited the day before. And the mangroves survive despite this highly changing environment, giving us the opportunity to learn from their adaptations.

There are different types of mangroves. Some deal with this continuous inward flow of salt by carrying it away from their roots in their sap and depositing it in their older leaves that will soon be shed. Others have leaves with glands that excrete the salt in very highly concentrated solutions.

The need for safe drinking water increases every day. Across the globe, four in ten people are affected by water scarcity.[46] That number will climb as the world's population continues to increase, resulting in serious health consequences.

---

45 Tributsch, H. (1984). *How Life Learned to Live*. Cambridge: The MIT Press.
46 10 Facts About Water Scarcity. *World Health Organization*. Retrieved June 4, 2008 from http://www.who.int/.features/actfiles/water/en/.

Companies like GE are taking lessons from these natural examples by building desalination stations that use a membrane technology to transform seawater and brackish water into fresh water, and for irrigation and industrial applications. GE's desalination stations are reclaiming more than 2 billion gallons of water a day, an amount equal to the daily water required by more than 150 million people.

Capturing water from natural sources is another way to address the scarcity of water, and the Namibian beetle does this well. It lives in the Namibian desert, one of the driest areas on earth. It survives by facing the wind and lifting its shell to trap the moisture from fogs created when cool waters off the Atlantic meet the warm landmass of the African coast. When enough drops coalesce into larger droplets, the water then rolls down the waxy troughs between the bumps on the beetle's back, reaching the beetle's mouth.

The British architectural designer Matthew Parkes mimicked this design by building a fog catcher for a hydrological center for the University of Namibia.[47] The building is made of an arched series of pods, behind a tall screen of nylon mesh. It faces the ocean and collects the fog in the mesh as it rolls in. When the mesh becomes saturated, gravity feeds the moisture into gutters that lead to underground cisterns, where the water is kept cool and safe from evaporation.

The need for such innovations is acute. The fog collectors are being sent to areas that receive only four- to eight-tenths of an inch of rainfall per year. Dr. Joh Henschel, of the Windhoek-based Namibian Desert Research Foundation, points out that fog water is sustainable and that it has been there for millions of years, and adds that collecting it is not taking anything away from the environment.

---

47   Kileen, M. (2002). An architect's water-collecting design mimics the insect world. Retrieved January 6, 2009 from http://www.metropolismag.com/html/ content_0502/ ob/ob05_0502. html

Rivaling the Namibian beetle in water-capturing skills is the Australian thorny red devil lizard, although it uses a different mechanism.

This lizard is not only an unusual source of inspiration, but is also one of the strangest creatures you have ever seen. It is four to six inches long, and is covered in thorny spikes and grooved skin. It has a knob that resembles a head on its back, which it exposes when threatened. This lizard's tongue is very sticky and fast-moving, though the rest of it moves quite slowly.

It collects water in an unusual way: It navigates through dewy landscapes and arranges for water to fall on it from its surroundings. It also uses tiny channels between the scales on its skin and legs to collect morning dew and water from damp sand, with the channels causing water to travel up by capillary action. This allows the lizard to suck in water from all over its the body, with the capillaries ending near its mouth.

Passive collection and distribution systems of naturally distilled water, like those described here, could help provide clean water and reduce the energy required to collect and transport it. Even the simple notion of a bumpy surface, like the skin of the thorny red devil, can teach us things about water conservation, something that we apparently have not learned well enough yet.

Flat surfaces like parking lots and cleared land for new housing construction are not environmentally advantageous. In fact, they exacerbate the flooding problems we now face in some areas because water pools and stagnates without slopes to aid in runoff.

In new housing sites we install huge water drainpipes below ground to take our water away after only one use. If we did not have the technology to purify and re-use water (which, of course, we do), we could still re-use much of our water, say from showers or baths, to water our lawns and gardens.

Fresh water is a precious commodity that should not be wasted. The drainage swale is a simple design that is a shaped and sloped depression in the surface of the soil that can be used to convey runoff to a desired location. Equally simple, yet useful, is the European model of capturing roof water used mostly for flushing toilets, washing and irrigation. It only takes the application of an ultraviolet filter or equivalent to uncontaminated roof water to turn it into safe drinking water.

So far I have given a number of diverse examples of innovation from nature, some of which can be replicated easily, others remain to be deciphered. They are but tiny specks in a large universe awaiting our discovery.

In the area of health and nutrition, a fascinating example is the eating behaviors of certain animals. But first, just imagine. Wouldn't it be nice if you no longer had to worry about which foods you should eat to stay slim and healthy? No more calorie-counting, or more enviously watching your colleague happily scarf down a triple-fudge sundae as you sadly nibble on your carrot and celery sticks willing your thighs to shrink? Even better, how about no more dealing with the guilt that comes with the morning after you have binged on food?

Well, mammals, birds and even bugs are known to naturally avoid dietary toxins and seek the healthiest food choices without any intervention to change their habits.

Rats make better nutritional choices in their food than the makers of rat food, as Dr. Curt P. Richter at Johns Hopkins University in Maryland found out. Richter gave rats rat chow separated into its component parts, including proteins, oils, fats, salts and sugars. Even when they were given unlimited quantities, the rats chose the components that enabled them to grow faster than rats fed the normal chow, but had few calories.[48] Perhaps it is safe to say that rats are immune from the affliction of having "eyes bigger than their bellies."

In another study, Dr. Kenneth Glander at Duke University in North Carolina, tested the food choices of the lemur, a primate found on the island of Madagascar.[49] He gave lemurs 10 leaves from local tree species like sweet gum that they had never seen before, with five of them containing substances that inhibited digestion. The lemurs were not fooled: They ate the good leaves and spit out the bad ones, while choosing a balance of leaves that had the highest nutrition content and digestibility.

Monkeys also have preferences and scientists have found that it is quality of the soil that determines them. Trees that grow in poor soil, where leaves are more difficult to grow, will increase the toxins in their leaves to repel the leaf-eating predators. Monkeys also are drawn to soil under some circumstances. Soil, generally, has many important minerals and clay, and when monkeys are sick, they will eat it. One of these minerals has kaolin, the active ingredient in Kaopectate, that neutralizes stomach acids.

There are many other examples in nature where living species self-medicate. Naturally occurring medicinal substances include reserpine from a tropical shrub for high blood pressure, diosgenin from wild yams in Mexico for contraceptive pills and digitalis from the purple foxglove, for congestive heart failure.

If all of this were not impressive enough, then there is the mind-boggling behavior of the mantled howler monkey, aptly named for the

---

48 Benyus, J. ibid (p. 152)
49 Glander, K. (1994). Non Human Primate Self-Medication with Wild Plant Foods. In Etkin, N. (Ed.) *Eating on the Wild Side: The Pharmacologic, Ecologic and Social mplications of Using Noncultigens*. (p. 227-239)

cacophonous territorial sounds it makes at dawn and dusk. It might seem outlandish to think that the female howler monkey engages in reproductive eating, which is effectively eating specific foods that affect the gender of the offspring. But birth records kept for 22 years, showing skewed ratios of males to females, suggest this is true. The normal ratio is usually 1:1, but Kenneth Glander from the Department of Biological Anthropology and Anatomy at Duke University, found that one female had four babies, all four males; another had nine babies, eight of them males; and a third had five babies, four of them females.[50]

It appears that the monkeys eat plants that can alter the electrical conditions in their reproductive tracts. The electrical environment is affected by acidic and alkaloid foods. A sperm carrying the female X chromosome is electropositive, while a sperm carrying a male Y chromosome is electronegative. Glander and his colleagues hypothesized that eating either an acidic or alkaloid food can block or enhance the charge of the X or Y chromosome.

What purpose does this serve? In evolutionary terms, survival and reproduction depend upon an even split of genders. If the population is low on females or males, then the mother may eat appropriately to correct that balance.

These awe-inspiring examples are both exciting and humbling. They are exciting because these masters of innovation are all around us, as if beckoning us to unravel their mysteries, yet these same masters of innovation are humbling because they perform their miracles in self-sustaining and life-enhancing ways.

---

50 ibid.

Janine Benyus, an American natural sciences writer and author of Bioimicry: Innovation Inspired by Nature, describes nine principles that resonate in the field of biomimicy. They are:

Nature runs on sunlight.
Nature uses only the energy it needs.
Nature fits form to function.
Nature recycles everything.
Nature rewards cooperation.
Nature banks on diversity.
Nature demands local expertise.
Nature curbs excesses from within.
Nature taps the power of limits.

In developing the mindset of an innovator, and by adhering to these principles in all that we do, we will learn to shift our current focus from mastery over nature to mastery within it. With such a life-respecting philosophy, we cannot fail.

There is another rich world of creativity and innovation from which we can also draw inspiration. It is invisible, but no less powerful. Like the natural world, it is immeasurable, vast and relatively unexplored. Unlike the science of biomimicry, it is not new, nor is it relatively unknown, but it is definitely underestimated and underexplored. It is the fertile world of the human mind, up next.

Part Two

Chapter 7

Metaphors in the Mind

Ask a woman if she likes to wear pantyhose and the likely answer is that she does not. If you asked her why, you would hear a number of opinions: "They are uncomfortable," "They feel like shrink-wrap," "They are cold in the winter and hot in the summer" or "They run as soon as you put them on." There are some women who feel that pantyhose would be better used as fan belts for cars in case of emergencies. A few women might say they like pantyhose, but it is rare for anyone to say that they love them.

These are the types of answers you would probably get if you did market research, whether in a focus group, telephone interview or a survey. If you were a pantyhose manufacturer, you might end there, having gotten the answers to your questions. But you would be wise to look deeper, deep into the human brain, where you would get useful information that would help you in truly understanding your consumer.

To get deep inside, you might – instead of simply asking questions -- ask women to collect pictures from magazines, catalogs and photo albums that represent their thoughts and feelings about wearing pantyhose.[51] The folks at DuPont, which manufactures fibers for women's hosiery, did exactly this. They conducted a market research study using this picture technique and found provocative results.[52]

Women brought pictures of trees being strangled by steel bands, fence posts wrapped in tight plastic and twisted telephone cords. There was no

51   Zaltman J. and Zaltman, L. (2008). *Marketing Metaphoria: What Deep Minds Reveals About the Minds of Consumers.* Massachusetts: Harvard Business School Publishing.
52   Pink, D. (1998). Metaphor Marketing. *Fast Company.* March 14

ambiguity there. Included in the choices were pictures of two African masks hanging on a bare wall, a luxury car, an ice-cream sundae spilled on the ground and a vase of flowers.

Glenda Green, market research manager at DuPont, further probed the women's thoughts in follow-up interviews. The woman who chose the fence posts wrapped in plastic said that hose made her feel thin and tall. The ice-cream sundae represented the embarrassment caused by the runs in pantyhose. The expensive car was associated with the feeling of luxury. Wearing pantyhose, some of the women said, made them feel sensual, sexy and more attractive to men.[53]

Subtleties related to sexual issues also surfaced, Green said. "Women would say, 'They make my legs feel longer.' Why is it important to have long legs? 'Men like long legs.' Why do men like long legs? 'They're sexy.' And eventually women would say they wanted to feel sexy to men. You don't get that in a straight interview."[54]

Precisely.

This technique, known as the ZMET technique,[55] is based on the premise that discovering people's spoken and visual metaphors is extremely important in learning their conscious and unconscious thoughts and feelings about a topic. The pictures participants bring to the interview are their metaphors in this case: serve as cues to their thinking process. During the interview, the interviewer probes the interviewee's thoughts to uncover any hidden meaning.

Sometimes we don't know what we know because knowledge can be deeply embedded in the brain. We have glimpses of it when we recall a fact or piece of information seemingly out of the blue. Something

---

53 Zaltman et al. ibid.
54 Pink, D. (1998). Ibid.
55 Zaltman, et al. ibid.

triggers the memory of it, although we are not always conscious of what the trigger was. Cognitive scientists have long known that human beings think in images and metaphors, not in words.

Literally, metaphor means language that directly compares seemingly unrelated subjects. For example, "all the world is a stage" is a metaphor that is easily understood. Using them in speech gives maximum meaning and encourages interpretation to stoke the mind to think of a wide array of possibilities. That is why creative writers use them to make the ordinary strange and the strange ordinary, making life more interesting. The Greek philosopher, Aristotle, believed that the use of metaphor was a sign of genius. He thought those who had the capacity to see resemblances between two different areas of existence and link them together were people of special gifts.

Metaphors, along with analogies, (which is the drawing of comparisons between independent parts) and similes, using figurative language to draw comparisons , are all effective techniques in innovating because they have the potential to spark leaps in thought to generate insight and discovery. At the very least, they can help us to clarify our thinking and communicate the meaning of what we're trying to say when words elude us.

A classic example of the use of metaphor is supplied by the German chemist Frederich Kekule, who discovered the ring shape of the benzene molecule. He was at a loss for words, yet described his breakthrough understanding of the molecule as "a snake biting its own tail" to explain the concept of the closed chain formation. The figure of speech illustrates how powerful a few words can evoke so much by painting the visual image through metaphors.

Another deliberate use of metaphor is the inkjet printer cartridge to improve the method for delivering drugs. Hypodermic needles are effective because they pass directly through the skin, but they are painful. They are often the method of choice for delivery because 95 percent of drugs in pill form are dissolved by stomach acid, making this form of delivery less than optimal.

By contrast, the cartridge has a series of tiny nozzles to spray drops of ink directly on the paper. By borrowing the design, HP has come up with the HP-Crospon skin patch, which contains about 150 micro-needles that deliver drugs.[56] The patch has a microchip that controls the dosage and administration time, which means that, depending on the patient's needs, multiple drugs can be given at once. Not only is the patch safer and more efficient than traditional injections, it is also painless to administer because the micro-needles do not penetrate the skin deeply enough to stimulate the pain receptors. From inkjet print cartridges to drug delivery systems -- who would have thought?

Who? People like Dean Cameron, the CEO of Biolytix, is who. An inventor and ecologist, he thought about applying the forest floor metaphor when he became disillusioned with the waste-water treatments on the market. He examined how a forest floor decomposes its litter and learned that worms, beetles, and microscopic organisms convert the waste into structured humus, the dark organic material in soil that is essential to the earth's fertility. The humus on the forest floor acts as a filter to turn the waste-water into pure water to irrigate the forest floor. There are no chemicals involved and the resulting water is safe for the environment.

Using these principles, he designed the Biolytix® filter, which decomposes debris on a river's edge to remove solid wastes from wastewater, and convert raw sewage, wastewater, and food waste into

---

56 Rotman, E. Skin Patch May Replace Traditional Injections. *The Future of Things*. 2007 04 Retrieved Jan. 2009 from http://thefutureofthings.com/news/1056/skin-patch-may-replace-traditional-injections.html.

high quality irrigation water on site. It uses 90 percent less electricity than most conventional systems and no chlorine.[57]

As you can see, metaphors to inspire innovation can be found anywhere, especially when you adopt the innovator's mindset. Applying metaphors in a deliberate way does not result in success every time; this new skill, like any other, takes practice, with the understanding that success is not guaranteed every time.

To get the most from working with a metaphor or image, you must break it down to its component parts and see if you can transfer those characteristics to the area where you are seeking new ideas.

For example, suppose you had a company that sells products and services related to IT (information technology). You have salespeople that call on customers across the country, and you are looking for ways to increase sales.

Now imagine a seahorse, for no other reason than my eyes randomly set upon a picture of one as I write this, and think of its characteristics. Here are some:

- They swim upright
- They steer with their heads and propel with their fins
- The females lay eggs into the males' pouches
- The males give birth to their young
- The babies are exact replicas of the adults

Now ask how you can transfer these characteristics to increasing sales.

- Seahorses swim upright – *The message is that the company will always be "above board" and reliable. Customers will, therefore, always be kept fully informed about all pertinent business matters.*

57   Biolytix Uses Nature, Not Machinery, to Treat Wastewater. *Biolytix Water Australia Pty. Ltd.* Retrieved January 6, 2009 from http://www.biolytix.com

A campaign can be built around reliability, for example, by structuring the company representatives in teams so that customers are always covered and they always have a conduit for information.

- They steer with their heads and propel with their fins – *A two-pronged sales approach can be devised, under which the first prong, "pre-sales" employees, steer the second prong, the salespeople, to potential new customers. The first group gathers knowledge, analyzing the market, assessing potential customers and gathering information that might be helpful in building a relationship. The second group is salespeople, using this knowledge in face-to-face meetings with customers. Going forward, members of the first group supply up-to-date market and competitive information to the members of the second group. All parties share in the bonus pool, meaning everyone has incentives to maintain quality customer relationships.*

- The females lay eggs into the males' pouches – *The software engineers (females) look for opportunities to design applications that fit into existing customer processes (the males' pouches). Avoiding duplication would reduce costs and sales would still be earned by maintaining the servicing of the application.*

- The males give birth to their young – *Begin a reward program for customers (males) who find new uses for (give birth to) or make improvements to products and services.*

- The babies are exact replicas of the adults – *Salespeople take replicas of their senior team in podcast messages to their customer meetings. The podcasts have messages from their company's president and other senior team members thanking them by name for their business. Customers get to see the rest of the team behind the products as well as getting a feeling of personal attention from the company's officers. The remainder of the podcast can have motivational information about the future of the company, its valued relationship with that customer and other important messages necessary to sustain an excellent relationship.*

As with many creative thinking tools, oftentimes the metaphors that seem the most unlikely to bring forth cause new ideas result in the best ones. Perhaps it is because that much more mental work is needed to connect the disparities and that means covering more conceptual space in the effort. The greater the mental distance traveled, the more the opportunity to find new ideas. Thinking does require effort and it is, indeed, tiring, but the good news is that just about anything can be used as an inspiration for innovation, even the most random event, as you will see next.

Exercises:

FIRST EXERCISE All right. You knew it would soon be your turn.

To get deep inside, take 15 minutes and go find a newspaper, catalog or magazine that represents your thoughts or feelings about one of these things:

1. Your computer

2. Running shorts

3. A key

Take the pictures, then explain your thoughts about the pictures. Write a sentence or six about your unconscious thoughts and feelings about the topic.

_____

_____

_____

_____

_____

_____

_____

No, you're not designing a replacement (computer, running shorts, key or whatever), but just for the exercise:

Take a second to bring the observations you just wrote down back to the concrete notion of how you might rethink the product, improve it, change it, accentuate positives and minimize negatives. For example: "Make a computer that doesn't make me think I'm dumb." "Make the running shorts more comfortable." "Make the key something you can't lose."

Ooh, gosh, we just talked about a key innovation: the newest keys are your iris or your fingerprint or your voiceprint, things you can't lose.

Hmmm, maybe we're on to something!

_____

_____

_____

_____

_____

_____

_____

Second Exercise

An exercise innovators may use is breaking down a metaphor or an image to its component parts, and then seeing if you can transfer those characteristics back to the area where you're seeking new ideas.

First, pick which area it is that you're seeking new ideas in._____

_____

Now, choose one of these three things, and do the same exercise you just read about with the seahorse:

1. A book —a book carries knowledge, which is ipso facto good. It is convenient, self-contained, portable, carries a warm emotional payload for most of us, and the form factor somehow makes us feel positive just looking at it. Also they are comfortable, familiar, etc.

2. An egg

3. A flower

First, list half a dozen characteristics.

_____

_____

_____

_____

_____

Then, transfer those characteristics to the problem. Really try to stretch your brain. You're learning how to use this technique, and it may not come easy.

_____

_____

_____

_____

_____

_____

If you want to, do it again. There's plenty of paper here, and it's only by practice that you develop the knowledge and proficiency with these techniques.

_____

_____

_____

_____

_____

_____

_____

_____

_____

_____

_____

_____

_____

_____

_____

_____

_____

You're done? O.K., pick some other seahorse (book, egg, flower). Whatever your eye lights upon. Do the exercise again.

_____

_____

_____

_____

_____

_____

_____

_____

_____

_____

_____

_____

_____

_____

_____

Third Exercise

A neuropsychiatrist named V.S. Ramachandran studies a condition called synesthesia, which is close to the world of metaphor. Like Aristotle, he thinks that the ability to see resemblances between two separate areas of existence is evidence of special gifts. Some of those who study synesthesia, like Dr. Ramachandran for example, have speculated that when we are born our brains are cross-wired, or highly interconnected, but that as the brain develops the cross-wiring is erased--except for those who have synesthesia, in which the evidence of cross-wiring may make a person feel that a letter has color, or a number has a personality.

Here is a description of synesthesia from Scientific American:[58]

When you eat chicken, does it feel pointy or round? Is a week shaped like a tipped-over _D_ with the days arranged counterclockwise? Does the note _B_ taste like horseradish? Do you get confused about appointments because Tuesday and Thursday have the same color? Do you go to the wrong train station in New York City because _Grand Central_ has the same color as the _42nd Street_ address of Penn Station? When you read a

---

58   Palmeri, T., Blake, R. and Marois,R. (2006). What is Synethesia? _Scientific American._
      Retrieved October 4, 2009 from http://www.scientificamerican/com /article.cfm?id-what-is-synethesia

newspaper or listen to someone speaking do you see a rainbow of colors? If so, you might have synesthesia.

Synesthesia is an anomalous blending of the senses in which the stimulation of one modality simultaneously produces sensation in a different modality. Synesthetes hear colors, feel sounds and taste shapes.

The estimated occurrence of synesthesia ranges from rarer than one in 20,000 to as prevalent as one in 200. Of the various manifestations of synesthesia, the most common involves seeing monochromatic letters, digits and words in unique colors: this is called grapheme-color synesthesia. One rather striking observation is that such synesthetes all seem to experience very different colors for the same graphemic cues. Different synesthetes may see *3* in yellow, pink or red. Such synesthetic colors are not elicited by meaning, because *2* may be orange but *two* is blue and *7* may be red but *seven* is green. Even more perplexing is that synesthetes typically report seeing both the color the character is printed in as well as their synesthetic color. For example, a blue colored numeral *5* is both blue (real color) and light green (synesthetic color).

Synesthetes report having unusually good memory for things such as phone numbers, security codes and polysyllabic anatomical terminology because digits, letters and syllables take on such a unique panoply of colors. But synesthetes also report making computational errors because *6* and *8* have the same color and claim to prejudge couples they meet because the colors of their first names clash so hideously. [59]

One famous synesthete, Vladimir Nabokov, wrote:

"The long *a* of the English alphabet (and it is this alphabet I have in mind farther on unless otherwise stated) has for me the tint of weathered wood, but a French *a* evokes polished ebony. This black group also

---

59   ibid.

includes hard *g* (vulcanized rubber) and *r* (a sooty rag being ripped). Oatmeal *n*, noodle-limp *l*, and the ivory-backed hard mirror of *o* take care of the whites. I am puzzled by my French *on* which I see as the brimming tension-surface of alcohol in a small glass. Passing on to the blue group, there is steely *x*, thundercloud *z*, and huckleberry *k*. Since a subtle interaction exists between sound and shape, I see *q* as browner than *k*, while *s* is not the light blue of *c*, but a curious mixture of azure and mother-of-pearl.[60]

This is a kind of metaphor/analogy/simile.

Most likely, if you are strongly a synesthete, this gave you a shock of recognition. If you are weakly a synesthete, you may have thought about this and haven't been able to put a name on it.

If you aren't sure, draw on your mind: make sure you're in a quiet place, and close your eyes for a while. Think of what correspondences you have. But before you do that, think of this:

--Do sounds or sights have feelings? (A harsh sound, a soft smile)

--Do letters have colors or feelings? Do numbers have colors or feelings?

--Does sadness make you see blue or feel blue?

What are the most obvious connections you see in the everyday world for synesthetes? Blue condolence cards, for example. Happy yellow suns on birthday cards. _____

_____

_____

_____

---

60 Nabokov, V. Speak in the Language of Rainbows. <http://www.greenchairpress.com/blog/p=203.>

_____

_____

_____

_____

People in New York City wear a lot of black. Is that synesthesia or pure hipster-ism?

_____

Free-associate a little about your own synesthesia, or if you don't have synesthesia, what you think it might feel like.

_____

_____

_____

_____

_____

Chapter 8

The Strange Bedfellows of Random Thoughts

Bill Bowerman, the head track and field coach at the University of Oregon for 24 years, had an exceptional ability to push his athletes to their peak, and his teams included 33 Olympic athletes and 64 All-Americans. He was also one of the founders of the Nike shoe company in 1964. One morning in 1971, while eating waffles for breakfast, Bowerman wondered if a waffle design on the sole of a running shoe would provide any competitive advantage. It was, perhaps, one of the most unlikely connections of thought in modern sporting history.

Bowerman borrowed his wife's waffle iron and created a pair of track shoes with a precise waffle pattern. Testing proved that the design did, indeed, enhance performance. The "Moon Shoe" was the first shoe in athletic history with such a pattern and was introduced in 1972. And the "Waffle Trainer" was then introduced in 1974, both of which helped to fuel Nike's explosive popularity and growth. Without that novel connection, Nike might today still be the small, moderately successful athletic shoe company it was before that fateful waffle breakfast.

This is an excellent example of how two disparate thoughts came together accidentally, when least expected, to yield a breakthrough. But like many stories that become the stuff of legends, some details are missing. Those moments leading up to that breakthrough thought were filled with many attempts to come up with ideas to improve the athletes' performance.

Ideas don't just occur out of the blue, although it sometimes seems that they do. The thinking that took place beforehand is what readies the mind to see new ideas. One famous illustration of this axiom, of course, is the popular tale of Newton sitting under an apple tree when an apple fell on his head -- and voila, the Universal Law of Gravity was born. That "aha," though, actually came after Newton had spent many hours pondering planetary motion.

What is interesting about these examples is that they illustrate the usefulness of incubation, a period of time spent diverting attention away from the focus. The mind continues to work on the focus, albeit not consciously. An unrelated stimulus, be it an event, sound or object, then triggers a connection in the mind, bringing it back to consciousness.

For many years, the importance of incubation wasn't well understood, but people who practiced it intuitively knew it was worthwhile, as in the case of George de Mestral, a Swiss inventor.

In 1941, de Mestral and his dog were hiking in the Swiss mountains. Throughout the day he had to disentangle sticky cockleburs from his pants and his dog's fur. He wondered why these pesky seedpods were so difficult to pull off. That evening he placed one under a microscope and found that its exterior was covered with lots of tiny hooks, which acted like hundreds of grasping hands. He wondered whether it would be possible to mimic nature and create a fastener for fabric. He did that and subsequently named it Velcro, using the first syllables of two French words: *velour* (velvet) and *crochet* (hook). But that isn't the end of the story.

De Mestral was an engineer who worked in a machine shop in Switzerland, and despite his training, it took another eight years to perfect his burr-clasping system. In 1952, he quit his job and got a loan to work on it. He found a way to make the hook side of the fabric, but he faced many challenges in trying to design the loop side of the fabric because the loops had to be in just the right spot to be fastened and unfastened many times. Frustrated, he went off to the mountains to clear his head. At a local barbershop, he watched the cutting and sliding motions of the barber's shears and it was then that he had his inspiration. He bought a pair of shears and trimmed the tops off the loops, thus creating hooks that would match up perfectly with the loops on the fabric, and used that idea to design the mechanization process.

As the story goes, some time later, De Mestral offered some advice to a group of executives: "If any of your employees ask for a two-week holiday to go hiking, say yes."

In brainstorming sessions I have run over the years, I always ask: Where do you get your best ideas? Invariably people say "in the shower," "at the gym," "on my way to work," and similar types of answers, but seldom do they say "at work." In our time-crunched world, it seems, many people feel they just don't have time to think. In a perfect world, we could take time away whenever we feel the need to let our thoughts incubate and get inspired. But that just isn't possible most of the time, nor is it a practical way to get ideas when you need them.

One of the greatest misconceptions about creative thinking is that it cannot be planned or systematically employed. This is not true. Using deliberate thinking methods that break the natural pattern of thinking, like simply pairing random thoughts, can significantly improve the chances of getting creativity towards innovation.

Leonardo da Vinci did this. He often forced himself to form new relationships between dissimilar subjects. In his art, he used random variations to design his famous caricatures and grotesque heads. He would start by listing a number of facial characteristics such as nose, eyes, mouth, ears, and then mix and match the different characteristics to form original and grotesque caricatures. In the area of science, Leonardo made the connection that sound travels in waves by connecting the sound of a bell with a stone hitting water.

Similarly, the physicist, Niels Bohr, believed that if you can hold opposite thoughts together while suspending judgment in your mind, then your mind moves to a new level. This is how he came up with the now-famous principle of complementarity that light is both a particle and a wave.

We can use the above examples as a blueprint and do this more systematically. In other words, force new connections in thinking by juxtaposing a random connection[61] with a focus.

Consider the case of a phone company in Australia years ago. Managers conducted a brainstorming session to come up with new ideas to boost revenues. They had considered increasing the cost of calls made at their public telephones, but a market sensitivity test revealed that customers already found the phones too expensive. If the company raised the cost per call, customers said, then they wouldn't use them as much. So the company was in a quandary until they tried this random connections technique.

A group of employees held a brainstorming sessions and were each given a list of randomly generated words, numbered one through to sixty, on a piece of paper. One participant was asked to pick a number between 1 and 60, without looking at the list. She blurted out "34," referring to her age. The group then looked at the list to see what word was beside the number 34. The word was "pipe." The question now was, what do you think of when you hear the word pipe? That led to the concept of lead.

---

61 de Bono, E. (1992). *Serious Creativity: Using the Power of Lateral Thinking to Create New Ideas.* New York: Harper Business

The next part of the task was to use the word "lead" to come up with an idea to increase revenues. Now came the freewheeling associating. It doesn't matter if the word "lead" means one thing to one person, and another to someone else, so long as it can send the discussion toward an idea to improve revenues.

Someone suggested putting pieces of lead into the handsets of the telephones to make them too heavy to hold for any length of time. That idea met with guffaws, raised eyebrows and blank stares -- but to everyone's surprise, it was the winning idea. One of the engineers convinced the rest of the group to design a phone with a heavy handset so customers would keep their conversations short and the phones would be freed for greater turnover. It wasn't a very customer-friendly solution, but given the technological limitations at the time, it achieved the objective.

If you cast your mind back to not so long ago when public phones were in greater use, you will recall that their design was not user-friendly: they had short, inflexible cords, and most booths had no seat. They were purposely built for utility more than comfort. The point is this: decide what you want to focus on and work toward that objective.

Note the structured process before the freewheeling thinking. It seems paradoxical that creative thinking would require a structured process, but it is, in fact, necessary, because creative thinking is a skill that can be developed and improved, and shouldn't be left to chance.

Randomness is the key to success in this technique, and it is appreciated only when one understands how the brain works.

Briefly, the brain is self-organizing so that all information that comes in through our five senses is automatically sequenced and categorized. It is not random. We must be able to make sense of what we are seeing, hearing, touching and experiencing, generally. It allows us to make sense of the world around us.[62]

If all the sensory information reaching your brain were weighted equally, you would be overloaded with data and you would not be able to make sense of the world. At every moment, we are sifting through mental clutter and external stimuli, navigating through endless distractions to focus and function normally. It is this ability that allows us to attend to the pertinent "foreground" information and relegate the rest to the "background."

We make sense of all that information with our patterning system in the brain. Think of it as a mental taxonomy, where patterns and connections are formed in the mind and expanded as we grow and learn our environment.

This patterning system is useful because it helps us recognize things. We see things with the help of our previous experiences. The problem with this is that it is difficult to break out of this patterning system and see things anew. A random association enables us to do just that.

One effective tool [63] to use when thinking gets stuck or stale is the random connections technique, which shakes up existing thought patterns.

Eric, a director of new product development for a soft-drink maker, realized this when he was looking for new ideas in one of his regular brainstorming sessions with a group of employees from across the company. Ideas were flowing, but they were mostly "me-too" ideas that were incremental improvements on the existing products. without intending to try a specific randomizing technique, his eyes happened to rest upon a nice garden outside of the conference room window, and he

---

62 ibid.
63 ibid.

immediately thought of the words "seed" and "pod". He asked his team to use these words to think of ideas.

From "seed" arose the idea of supplying customers with the product in the form of seeds. The group didn't take that literally, but it prompted a similar idea: supplying the product in the form of a concentrate. It resonated because it had multiple benefits: it would reduce the cost of shipping heavy containers, eliminate the need for refrigeration and reduce the amount of packaging required, giving it a welcome eco-friendly advantage.

From the word "pod" the group came up with another idea: a "NutriPod" unit, similar to a water cooler, but with more options like a vending machine, for customers who would buy only the concentrate. They could then mix it with the water in the unit, or another liquid of their choice, and control the sweetness.

Armed with many good ideas, a few weeks later the group got together again to continue the brainstorming and build on what they had. By then, discussions had begun with potential partners in the food and nutraceutical industries. The NutriPod was shaping up to be a multifunctional unit that not only stocks complementary, tasty products, but can also offers food customized to a person's nutritional needs because it has been programmed to match a nutritional profile.

As is often the case with innovation, boundaries of any sort – and in this case, between industries and markets – become blurred. This endeavor began in the soft-drink market, but moved into health and nutrition, tapping into the specialized scientific field of nutragenetics, where they learned that genetic profiles can be assessed to determine one's unique nutritional needs. And if that wasn't exciting enough, there is another benefit to owning a NutriPod. You need not ever visit a grocery store to replenish its contents, because the automatic inventory control sends a message to the store over the Internet. Your groceries are then delivered to your door, the ultimate convenience.

All of this came from the random words "seed" and "pod." Of course, the NutriPod will need a new name to portray its many attributes, but that's part of the fun in creativity. Sometimes you never know where you'll end up, but if you're prepared, it can be a very profitable distance ahead.

One could argue that these ideas might have surfaced without this random thought process and, indeed, that's possible. But my experience suggests that is unlikely, because we tend often to begin with what we already have and then try to improve it. This incremental-improvement approach often leads to improvements that are foreseeable. If you can see them, so can your competitor, and that won't give you a window of opportunity to get ahead of the competition. The random connections technique gets you away from incrementalism and into whole new areas of thinking. It won't work every time, but it can improve the likelihood of generating new and possibly breakthrough ideas more often.

Random connections is one of the easiest thinking tools to employ. With practice, you realize that whatever random stimuli you use – words, sounds, pictures or objects – the one that seems furthest away from your goal is the one that yields you the best ideas. That's what happened when Gary, an office manager in an insurance company, held a meeting with his team to tackle tardiness. People always showed up late for meetings, and this had become not just a habit but even part of the corporate culture. Managers had tried techniques to change this habit, such as charging $5 to latecomers or making them get up and sing a song in public, but that backfired. Apparently, there were some folks who secretly hoped they could be "discovered" and used this as an auditioning forum. They intentionally showed up late, turning the meetings into mini-karaoke sessions that were even more disruptive than the tardiness.

In Gary's office, he proudly displayed a picture of a firefly drawn by his 5-year-old son. They decided to use it as a random picture, focusing on the fly's ability to blink in the dark. The question then was "How can we get people to come to meetings on time?"

Someone came up with the idea of having the lights in meeting attendees' offices start blinking 10 minutes before the meeting, giving them notice to head out. That idea, in turn, led the IT department to configure the electronic calendar system to blink a large message over the computer screen 10 minutes before meetings.

On-time attendance did improve, although there are still people who will inevitably be late because of circumstances beyond their control. They turned this negative into a positive by another association with the firefly -- being kept in the dark. The original thought was that to reduce disruption by latecomers, those latecomers should be kept in the dark. In other words, they were not to be told by anyone what they had missed. That led to the thought that perhaps not everyone should be "in the light" or actually invited to various meetings.

It is well known in the corporate world that often people are invited to meetings unnecessarily and that meetings, quite often, are unproductive, unfocused and, consequently, time-wasting. What has now become part of this corporate culture is a reminder to invite only those employees necessary for a meeting. If an employee feels that he has nothing to add, he has the "right of refusal" to attend. This is perhaps not a breakthrough idea, but creative thoughts come in big and small sizes.

Forcing new, random connections in thinking, as we have seen, can be done in many ways. And yet the notion of randomness is often underestimated and, therefore, not used to its full potential.

In practice, what usually happens is that during a brainstorming session the thinking gets stale and the ideas start to sound the same. You may hear new words, but the same messages are underneath. That is the time to bring in a random connections exercise.

If you simply take a list of randomly generated words, scan that list and then choose one at random to work with, you have just violated the randomness rule.

How can that be? Because even though you may do your best to choose a word that appears random, your brain is always at work, constantly scanning the environment, as it were, making those connections so that your world makes sense. It mostly occurs below your conscious awareness. Despite your best intentions, you are actually choosing a word that seems most likely to connect to what you are doing at the time. It is part of your neurological wiring.

This wonderful neurological system can be seen in a young child, for example, who lives in a household with a family dog. The dog is a big, black Labrador. A cat passes by outside, and she points at it, declaring "dog." She is not yet able to distinguish the cat from a dog, but she is still able to distinguish the cat from a chair. This, in effect, is a neurological anchor that serves as an organizing principle of the mind.[64] The anchors enable you to form general concepts from the perception of individual facts. From early on, children can recognize that dogs, cats and rabbits belong to a different category than say, chairs, tables and plates.

In more fully appreciating the difficulty in choosing something randomly, it turns out that there is an even more complex function in the brain that allows the mind to connect two or more separate facts. We

---

64　See Newberg, A., D'Aquili, E. and Rause, V. (2001). *Why God Won't Go Away: Brain Science & the Biology of Self-Belief.* New York: Ballantine for an interesting discussion of the brain's functions based on a long-term investigation and multiple brain imaging studies on meditating Buddhists and Franciscan nuns at prayer.

are able to generate scientific theories, philosophical assumptions and explanations, generally, because of this neurological function. In essence, we can use facts to derive theories to explain something. The theories are not known to be true as they are abstractions from the facts, but forming a theory is a way of connecting the dots with your best assumptions.

Likewise, when you find yourself in a situation where you are not generating theories, but rather trying to understand the random information in front of you – in this case, the list of random words – the cognitive imperative compels us to form a connection to make sense of it.

So, in the act of scanning the list of random words, in the back of your mind you are aware that you are doing this because you are seeking some new ideas for an issue you are trying to solve. Without your conscious awareness, your brain is already trying to make sense of what you are seeing by striving to form connections. This is what causes you to pick the word that feels closest to what you are trying to do.

For instance, if you are looking for ways to build efficiencies in your manufacturing operations, you might come across the word "scissors." The obvious connection is "cut" – cut costs, cut materials, cut whatever. It feels right because it makes sense. Moreover, we naturally are drawn more toward that with which we are familiar than we are toward what is different. The result is that nothing really new is likely to come from that session, because cutting costs is a standard solution.

"Fungus," "turtle" and "dandruff" are three words that, if introduced to this brainstorming session, would elicit moans, sneers and general disbelief, but would actually have a greater likelihood of generating new and different ideas for the manufacturing process.

Any words, or whatever stimuli you choose to use, that are so unrelated on account of their extreme disconnection, require a greater mental distance for you to cross in your efforts to connect them. It is much the same as changing the route you take to work every day. The old route has become routine. You don't see much new, and stop noticing things you take for granted.

But when you change to a new route, you not only see more, but you also see new things that heighten your awareness. It is an experience of greater mental alertness that promotes more active thinking than normal. Trying to connect the most unlikely random words forces you to engage in these mental gymnastics. You cover more ground by having to try out new connections in thinking, and a greater quantity of thinking will result in a greater likelihood of new ideas.

Exercise: Random Connections

Suppose you are looking for some new ideas for improving your staff's morale during these tough economic times. Using "goose" as the random word, I immediately think of the word "duck". Then I try and come up with some ideas with this word that will improve staff morale: Random Connection:

Duck

- Ducks have ducklings. Lighten the mood in the office by periodically holding an ugly outfit day (associated with ugly duckling).

- In a newsletter, Intranet or similar medium, have employees share their customer experiences with the rest of the company, under the good, the bad and the ugly. The good experiences can be an opportunity to share best practices, the bad an opportunity to learn from one another's mistakes, and the ugly can be the embarrassing experiences that others would find funny.

- Now what examples can you come up with?

  _____

- ???

  _____

- ???

  _____

You can never predict which creative thinking tools will yield the best ideas, but having multiple tools to choose from will increase the quantity of ideas you can build upon. Thinking can become stale quickly, so changing the momentum by changing to another thinking tool will keep the ideas flowing. Wishing for a perfect world is another fun tool that will do just that. As you will see next, your wishes can be turned into practical ideas with just a little structure.

Chapter 9

It Starts With a Wish

Two little words can change reality. They set you on a path of exploration in your mind and if you back them up with the determination to follow them through, they can change the world. Those words are "what if." What if I could make the world a better place? What if I could take care of everybody at a higher standard of living than many have ever known? What if all of humanity had the option to become enduringly successful? These were lofty "what if" questions from a man who was penniless and uneducated. They were asked nonetheless, and they changed the world.

Bucky horrified his parents by being expelled from Harvard a number of times and then failing to graduate.[65] His parents, wealthy New England folks with a long history of Harvard graduates in their lineage, worried about their son's future. Bucky did not seem to know what he wanted to do.

Without a solid university education, they thought, his future was uncertain at best. But Bucky did know one thing. He was in love, and he decided to marry his sweetheart. Shortly thereafter he joined the U.S. Navy. The experience he gained as a communications officer and gunboat commander turned out to be a determining influence in his life and work. After leaving the Navy in 1922, he co-founded a construction company and set about learning design and architecture, but the company did not do well.

---

65   See fascinating facts about R. Buckminster Fuller inventor of the Geodesic Dome in 1954 in
     http://www.ideafinder.com/history/inventors/fuller.htm and Buckminser Fuller Institute
     http://www.bfi.org.

He found himself out of a job not long after. Around that time, he also lost his four-year old daughter, Alexandra, to complications from polio and spinal meningitis. He was devastated. He felt responsible for her death because the family's house was cold and drafty, and he often wondered if that had made her condition worse. Jobless, bankrupt and depressed, he contemplated suicide, and even walked to the shores of Lake Michigan to drown himself. It was there that it struck him that his life belonged not to himself, but to the universe. He decided to devote his life to others. He started by asking "What if I could devise a new, more efficient, way of housing mankind?"

It took some time, but Bucky, more formally known as Buckminster Fuller, ended up gaining an international reputation for his work in lightweight, inexpensive and speedily constructed housing. His many accomplishments include 25 registered U.S. patents, 28 books and 47 honorary doctorates as well as numerous other awards, including a 1969 nomination for the Nobel Peace Prize.[66]

One of his most notable achievements was the geodesic dome (a "geodesic" line on a sphere is the shortest distance between any two points). The dome consists of self-bracing triangles in a pattern that uses the least material possible to enclose a space, delivering many benefits. The dome's low surface-to-volume ratio means that heat loss is greatly reduced and it is less affected by potentially damaging winds. The design also has a significant advantage over traditional building construction in that the larger the dome, the stronger, lighter and less expensive per unit of volume for its size.[67]

---

66   *R. Buckminster Fuller: Inventory, Designer, Architect, Theorist (1895-1983)* Retrieved
     January 9, 2009 from http://www.designmuseum.org/design/r-buckminster-fuller
67   ibid.

This type of "against all odds" story is always heartwarming and inspiring, but this story serves another purpose. Buckminster Fuller's inventions followed some tragic incidents in his life. His anger and sorrow eventually infused him with a passionate desire to help others.

Strong emotions, when turned in a positive direction, can be the driving force that will enable you to persevere when the going gets tough. History is replete with similar stories.

In the everyday world of business, where we strive to compete by innovating and where emotions are neutral, "what if" questions tend not to elicit the same level of drive to explore and solve. In the business world, these types of questions are generally entertained as casual musings and taken less seriously because they often depart from our known reality. The consequence is that they get discarded, and the seeds of potentially good ideas are lost. But it does not have to be this way.

Asking "what if" questions can become a productive and exciting exercise when you understand how the brain works and why this type of thinking is valuable. At the neurological level, when we are processing information, we think in a linear series of thoughts so that each thought is connected to another thought. We look for patterns and connections, and this allows us to make sense of our environment.

This is a fundamental need in all of us. It is so strong that even when there are neurological memory deficits, for example, caused by a stroke or other type of head trauma, a patient will make up an answer to a question he does not know. It is not a deliberate lie. In such a case, the confabulation is a person's attempt to escape the perplexity by stating a hypothesis that he or she mistakes for truth.[68] In other

---

68 Rhawn, J. "Confabulation and Delusional Denial: Frontal Lobe and Lateralized Influences." Brain Research Laboratory, Neurobehavioral Center. Reprinted from: *Journal of Clinical Psychology* 42 (1986): 845-860.

words, a patient who is unable to remember will make up an answer to a question believing it to be a truth. He is unaware that he does this. It happens because of our strong need to make sense of the world and make connections.

This sense-making need of ours is beneficial in brainstorming, especially when prefaced by the words "what if." Entertaining "what if" moves us forward in the mind to areas outside of the normal connections. The nature of "what if" asks us to consider something new and we immediately try to make connections, sometimes coming up with novel thoughts. It won't always work, but it can, and the more practice you get, the greater the likelihood that new ideas will come.

Researchers at Intel know the power of "what if" questions well. Justin Rattner, the chief technology officer at Intel, asked: "What if machines had a small amount of intelligence, and they could assemble themselves into various shapes that were capable of movement or locomotion? If you had enough machines like this, you could create arbitrary shapes and have the assembly of machines that could take on any form and move in arbitrary ways."[69] He was referring to the concept of shape-shifting.

The idea is to figure out how to harness millions of miniature robots, called catoms, and program them to change shape as needed. The catoms, which are now measured in inches, would one day be the size of a grain of sand and they could be manipulated with electromagnetic forces to cling together in various 3D forms.

This research is an expansion on a project by Seth Goldstein, associate professor at Carnegie Mellon University, and it is becoming a real

---

69   Gaudin, Sharon. "Intel shows off research into tiny robots that can be programmed to take on the shape of anything. (Computerworld (US). 2008 10:49:00 https://www.techworld. com.au/ article/258085/ intel_sees_future_shape-shifting_robots_wireless_power

possibility. Now the catoms have microprocessors in them that attract or repel one another via electromagnetism or the use of electrostatic charges, says Rattner. In essence, the catom is programmable matter.

Jason Campbell, a senior researcher at Intel, says that catoms will change the way people interact with computers and other devices in significant ways.[70] "The cell phone is too large to comfortably fit in your pocket," Campbell says.[71] The keyboards on P.D.A.s are too small to type on and the devices' screens are too small to view movies on. Catoms can be manipulated to take on the shape of the device needed at the moment. Keyboards can be enlarged for text messaging and then formed into smaller units to fit inside a pocket when not used.

According to both Campbell and Rattner, the biggest obstacle to making this happen right now is figuring out how to make the catoms think like a swarm. But as we saw in Chapter 3, if companies such as Air Liquide and Southwest Airlines can design computer algorithms based on the swarm behaviors of ants to aid their businesses, it is only a matter of time before this obstacle will be overcome. These researchers believe that shape-shifting devices will exist in less than 10 years.

Let's pose a what-if question about global warming. What if we could use shape-shifting to improve our ability to withstand changing weather patterns? What if you could build buildings to withstand extreme storms? What would they look like? Immediately your mind begins to look for answers to these questions.

How can buildings change their shape? Look no further than Chicago, where buildings are being designed with an exoskeleton, known

---

70 Intel shows off research into tiny robots that can be programmed to take on the shape of anything. *Sharon Gaudin* (Computerworld (US)) Retrieved 25/08/2008 10:49:00 from https://www.techworld.com.au/ article/258085/intel_sees_future_shape-shifting_robots_ wireless_power

71 Ibid.

as an actuated tensegrity superstructure. These structures are made of rods and wires manipulated by pneumatic "muscles", that let wind blow through it and gives every room access to sunlight.[72] The building swivels and twists gently in the wind to control its center of gravity, reducing harmful shaking and swaying. These shape-shifting responsive structures function like living systems that work with the force of natural energy, not against it, and they do not consume a lot of energy in the process.

Architects can now build taller buildings on land, and in the near future, they will be able to build these buildings in water. There will be huge platforms built in the sea to hold these structures, where people can work while the energy from waves can be exported through them.

Building more on the shape-shifting concept, in 2010 Dubai became the home of the "world's first building in motion" with 80 floors that each rotate independently at different speeds.[73] This will give every inhabitant a 360 degree view. It will have 79 wind turbines that will generate electricity for itself as well as the surrounding building. Each floor of the tower would rotate independently on voice command, allowing the building to constantly change shape. Its eco-advantage is that the skyscraper itself could be built entirely from prefabricated parts, resulting in huge cost savings.

When a breakthrough concept such as shape-shifting occurs, it is useful to take that concept and cross-pollinate it using the "what if" approach. Then continue to ask the "what if" questions and see where your thinking takes you. Borrowing ideas in one area and applying them in another is called cross-pollination.

---

72 Irvine, D."Buildings Get Wise To The Future." 2006. CNN.com. 28 Retrieved Feb. 2009 from http://www.cnn.com/2006/TECH /science/ 09/08/smart.buildings/index.html
73 "Dubai 'Shape-Shifting Skyscraper' Unveiled." 2008.28 Retrieved Feb. 2009. from http://www.cnn.com/WORLD/meast/06/25/ duibai.tower/ index.html

For example, what can you do with these "what if" questions:

- What if we could shape-shift land so crops can be changed back and forth, reducing the amount of land required altogether?

- What if we could eliminate poverty around the world by shape-shifting restaurants?

- What if we could shape-shift food sources?

- What if we could shape shift water sources to go from wet areas to dry areas?

The apparent loftiness of these questions subsides as you force yourself to consider the possibilities. You adopt the innovator's mindset, with the attitude that even if the idea does not work in its totality, something can be extracted from the suggestion.

In investigating the first question, shape-shifting land might seem ridiculous, but we can extract that concept of it and explore the possibility of shape-shifting as a concept rather than a reality. Bio-intensive farming techniques, practiced first in Japan and now elsewhere, are examples of applying the concept of shape-shifting. The Japanese examples have a few models.

One model is the Fukuoka "do-nothing" system of organic farming where a quarter acre of land can yield 22 bushels of rice and 22 bushels of winter grains with only one or two workers working only a few days a week to hand-sow and harvest a crop.[74] What makes this possible is a well-designed sequence of plantings that provide weed control, composting and other services automatically. There are other models that integrate many kinds of food production, such as vegetables, fish, rice, pigs, ducks, etc., in a sophisticated quasi-ecosystem that recycles its own nutrients through plant – animal interactions.[75]

It is encouraging to find that an answer to your "what if" question already exists because it is a validation that your thinking is on a good track. It is also a green light to go forward. Just asking the question primes your internal radar.

- What if we could shape-shift traffic jams to reduce congestion?

  _____

- What if we could change the shape of our cars to fit our needs?

  _____

- What if we could change a one-seat car into a six-seat car and then change it back again?

  _____

74   Hawkins, P., Lovins, A. and Lovins, L. *Natural Capitalism*. New York: Little, Brown & Co., 1999
75   ibid.

It did not take long to find a shape-shifting concept car made by BMW, called the GINA (geometry and functions in *N* adaptations -- the *N* representing an infinite number).[76] This car is wrapped in a spandex-like fabric stretched over a movable frame that allows shape changes. The fabric is resilient, durable and water resistant, and the owner can change the body shape with the car's electric and hydraulic systems. The fabric hiding the headlights opens like eyelids when needed; the front grill widens for cooling. The rocker panels, at the bottom of the side panels, change to improve airflow, and a spoiler rises at the rear. This car is light-weight and fuel-efficient.

What is particularly interesting about this car is that BMW does not plan to manufacture it for consumers. Instead, the car is intended to steer creativity and research in new directions.[77] In effect, this is a visual example of a "what if." It is not an end in itself, but rather a stepping-stone to new areas of thinking. Now think of how you can borrow this idea and apply it in your life or work.

Obviously, sometimes you will not find the answers to your "what if" questions, but just asking makes it easier for your mind to enter new territories. Continuously asking this type of question also ensures that you will not lapse into the take-it-for-granted style of thinking that we learn as we strive to control our time and achieve our goals. It is this type of inquisitiveness that we must reclaim from our childhood. "What if" that were possible?

---

76 Squariglia, C. BMW Builds a Shape-Shifting Car Out of Cloth. Autopia, 2008. Retrieved April 26,2009 from http://blog.wired.com/cars/2008/06/ bmw-builds-a-ca.html>
77 ibid.

Chapter 10

Broaden Your Thinking with M.F.C.

The audience in the conference room was a sea of white. There were 32 men there, each wearing the white floor-length robe called a dishdasha and a white headdress, and two women in the head-to-toe silky black cloaks called abayas. It was mid-morning on a Sunday and a normal workday here in Kuwait City. Weekends there are Thursdays and Fridays.

The office building was a non-descript eight-storey, grey building in the city center. Surrounding it was a landscape that felt colorless. The broken sidewalks and ill-defined parking spaces at the side belied the high standard of living that most Kuwaitis lived.

There was a lot to cover in this four-day innovation program, but you'd never have known it by the casual nature of what was transpiring in the room. There were frequent interruptions, with attendees entering and leaving the room. Sidebar conversations were occurring in a few corners, where some men were holding hands with each other and chatting. I found it a bit unusual and more than a little irritating.

It wasn't until a few days later that I had learned that the multiple conversations during the session were not a sign of deliberately rude behavior, as I had assumed. This was a polychronic society, in which greater emphasis is placed on relationships and events than on time commitments. Interruptions, changing plans and multiple events occurring at the same time were the norm.

I had been invited to deliver a creativity and innovation program to some managers in a customer services company and I was eager to work in a culture that I knew nothing about. But it was turning out to be more challenging than I had imagined.

124

I had read quite a bit on Kuwaiti culture in an attempt to make the experience enjoyable and productive for everyone. I learned that it was acceptable for me to dress in Western clothes as long as I didn't accentuate my waist in any way, and kept my arms and legs covered. Adhering to that was easy. Being awakened by the call to prayer at 3:30 a.m. took a bit of getting used to. It was a very different and interesting culture indeed.

My host had reminded me not to initiate a handshake with any fundamentalist Muslim man in the session.

"How would I recognize one?" I had asked.

"They always have a beard," said she, "and their robes are a few inches shorter at the front. Avoid eye contact with them as well."

So far, so good. No social blunders, but the interruptions were getting on my nerves. Standing at the flipchart, I asked for ideas on how to make the travel experience better for their customers.

"Segregate the sexes," said one of the fundamentalist Muslim men.

"Better yet, let the women stay at home," said another "and definitely no alcohol either."

"Yes," I assured them, "but outside of Kuwait, the Westerners will want some of that."

The moderate Muslims shook their heads in agreement. The few fundamentalist men in the group grimaced. There were a few chuckles, and it was then that I recognized that they were having some fun with me.

"Give me your perfect world scenarios," I said. "Tell me what would make you have the ultimate travel experience, if you could have anything you wanted without any limitations."

"I'd like to arrive at every travel destination knowing how to speak the local language fluently," said one of the women.

"I'd like to just be there when I want, without having to travel to and from at all." said another. Finally, the ideas were starting to flow. They were getting more and more illogical and just what I wanted. Now it was time to apply M.F.C. "Mine For Concepts."

First, assume that everything said in a brainstorming session is at least the seed of another idea. If the idea stated is impractical or illogical, treat it as only a starting point or stepping stone. Never discard it. Instead, ask this: what is the concept behind that idea?

The terms concept and idea are often used interchangeably, but they are not the same thing. To quickly tell the difference between them, and avoid getting too technical about it, an idea is specific whereas a concept is broad. Incentive is a concept because there are many ways you can incentivize. A $100 dinner certificate, a free lunch or a public acknowledgement of your good work are specific ideas in providing incentives. Penalty is a concept. Charging $5 for tardiness at company meetings is an idea, as are paying extra interest for late payments and having to do extra work for no pay.

Concepts underlie ideas, and there may be many concepts under one idea. Providing television entertainment at the checkout counter in a supermarket is an idea that has two concepts underlying it. It is both a reward to the customers (at least those who like the entertainment) and also a method of time distortion to keep customers engaged so they do not notice the time they are waiting to check out.

One of the greatest benefits to mining for concepts is that it breaks the linear thinking that arises in idea-generating sessions. When a new idea arises, what follows are improvements and modifications on that idea because building upon an idea is the easiest way to brainstorm. It is valuable, but limiting, because the ideas become simply more of the same.

In contrast, mining for concepts will help generate qualitatively different ideas.

The idea of the television at the supermarket checkout is a good example. If we asked for more ideas under the concept of rewarding the customer, we could get more ideas on things to give at the checkout counter, such as magazines, newspapers and other products customers could read while waiting.

If we asked for more ideas under the concept of time distortion, however, new areas of thinking open, such as providing headphones and seats for customers to listen to taped guided imagery for stress reduction, or computer monitors for customers to view short podcasts on a subjects of their choice. Concepts help change the direction of thinking.

Returning to the Kuwait experience, we start by asking if segregating the sexes is an idea or a concept? It is an idea because it is specific. Now ask: what is the concept or concepts behind it? One concept is segregation or separation of the genders. Other concepts are protection of the genders and customized travel routes for each gender where female and male needs are separately met. We do not know what concept drove the segregation idea initially, but it does not matter. We are looking only for fodder to generate more alternatives from the original idea. From each of those concepts, we can now generate more ideas.

From segregate the sexes, the group worked with the concept of protection of the genders, interpreting protection as protecting travelers from making any cultural faux pas. Group members came up with the idea of providing travelers with a pocked-sized sheet of cultural do's and don'ts for the areas they served. It was an inexpensive value-add that their customers appreciated.

From the idea of arriving at every travel destination knowing how to speak the local language fluently, the concept of education was culled.

The group expanded on the cultural tips with the idea of lessons on language, food, history and other information on the destination country on DVDs that travelers could watch during transit. Group members learned in the session not to reject an idea based on the impossibility of achieving absolute fluency, but rather to take such an idea as a starting point. The concept of education opened up all kinds of avenues to generate more logical ideas.

Getting there without having to travel in between led to more interesting ideas. Obviously, you cannot enable travelers to just get there without the time spent in between, but you can always give the impression of getting there with minimal waste of time. The group extracted the concept of time distortion, and then generated ideas of how to distort time so the travelers were not aware of the time they were in transit. Ideas flowed: video games, virtual reality headphones, massages. The list was nearly endless, and it led to further discussions on new partnerships with potential service providers.

This technique is often overlooked because of the tendency to quickly capture only logical ideas, accept or reject them, and then move on. It is a sign of our culture of instant gratification.

Good idea? Check -- keep it. Bad idea? Ignore it or cross it off the list, and keep moving.

Living in our time-restricted world exacerbates this tendency. Re-visiting ideas by mining for concepts, however, is a valuable exercise because it causes you to think about your thinking by getting underneath your thoughts. You can literally double the number of ideas with this technique, and in the world of creative thinking, quantity is more important than quality. It's easier to improve something already there than it is to generate totally new ideas, so make this a regular part of your innovation program wherever you can.

In brief:

1. Is it a concept or idea? If it is broad, it is likely a concept. (If it is specific, it likely is an idea.)

   _____

2. If it is a concept, what are some ideas that could be used to achieve it?

   _____

3. If it is an idea, what are some concepts behind it?

   _____

4. How many ideas can you generate from each of the concepts.?

   _____

Chapter 11

Fun with Morphology

The spotlight shines on the magician's assistant.[78] The woman in the tiny white dress is a luminous beacon of beauty radiating from the stage to the audience. The Great Tomsoni announces he will change her dress from white to red. On the edges of their seats, the spectators strain to focus on the woman, burning her image deep into their retinas. Tomsoni claps his hands, and the spotlight dims ever so briefly before flaring in a blaze of red. The woman is awash in a flood of redness.

Whoa, just a moment there! Switching color with the spotlight is not exactly what the audience had in mind. The magician stands at the side of the stage, looking pleased at his little joke. Yes, he admits, it was a cheap trick; his favorite kind, he explains devilishly. But you have to agree, he did turn her dress red -- along with the rest of her.

Please, indulge him and direct your attention once more to his beautiful assistant as he switches the lights back on for the next trick. He claps his hands, and the lights dim again; then the stage explodes in a supernova of whiteness. But wait! Her dress really has turned red. The Great Tomsoni has done it again!

The trick and its explanation by Thompson (a k a the Great Tomsoni) reveal a deep intuitive understanding of the neural processes taking place in the spectators' brains -- the kind of understanding that our neuroscientists can appropriate for their own benefit.

Here's how the trick works. As Thompson introduces his assistant, her skintight white dress encourages spectators to assume that nothing

---

78   Reproduced with the consent of Scientific American

-- certainly not another dress -- could possibly be hiding under the white one. That reasonable assumption, of course, is wrong. The attractive woman in her tight dress also helps to focus people's attention right where Thompson wants it -- on her body. The more they stare at her, the less they notice the hidden devices in the floor, and the better adapted their retinal neurons become to the brightness of the light and the color they perceive.

During Thompson's patter after his little "joke," each spectator's visual system is undergoing a brain process called neural adaptation. The responsiveness of a neural system to a constant stimulus (as measured by the firing rate of the relevant neurons) decreases with time. It is as if neurons actively ignore a constant stimulus to save their strength for signaling that a stimulus is changing. When the constant stimulus is turned off, the adapted neurons fire a "rebound" response known as an after discharge.

In this case, the adapting stimulus is the red-lit dress, and Thompson knows that the spectators' retinal neurons will rebound for a fraction of a second after the lights are dimmed. The audience will continue to see a red afterimage in the shape of the woman. During that split second, a trap door in the stage opens briefly, and the white dress, held only lightly in place with Velcro and attached to invisible cables leading under the stage, is ripped from her body. Then the lights come back up.

Two other factors help make the trick work. First, the lighting is so bright just before the dress comes off that when it dims, the spectators cannot see the rapid motions of the cables and the white dress as they disappear underneath the stage. The same temporary blindness can overtake you when you walk from a sunny street into a dimly lit shop. Second, Thompson performs the real trick only after the audience thinks it is already over. That gains him an important cognitive advantage -- the spectators are not looking for a trick at the critical moment, and so they slightly relax their scrutiny.[79]

Our minds work not with random bits of information, but rather in patterns, stories and cohesive connections that help us to see in wholes rather than in parts. Neural adaptation is responsible for some of the trick, but not all of it. This trick is also a good illustration of the interplay between seeing and thinking.

We are directed by the magician to see the woman, and we are attracted by her visual appeal, the least of which is her dress. Throughout the dress change, we see what we think is the whole scene, but we do not see the clues of the changing lights and cables simply because our attention is pulled away from these.

If we still had a need to make sense of what we were looking at, we would not be so easily diverted. Instead, we would scan the environment for bits of information to fill in the missing pieces and overlook those bits that do not fit. Here the scene of the woman in a nice dress is a complete message. Her attractiveness keeps our attention, so we do not look for more cues, sometimes overlooking pertinent details. We may see them, but we don't think about them, relegating them to below consciousness.

In magic shows and other forms of entertainment, this selective perception is a welcome escape. In the world of creative thinking, it is the diametric opposite of what you want – especially if you are seeking to develop the mind of an innovator in designing new products or services. Seeing all of what is in front of you has its advantages, but first you must do some meta thinking, in other words, think about what you are thinking, and how you are thinking.

---

79 Martinez-Conde. S. and Macknik, S.L. "Magic and the Brain: How Magicians Trick the Brain." *Scientific American* 24 Nov 2008. Reproduced with Permission from Scientific American.

An art teacher says this so well when she instructs her students in realist art class: "Draw what you see, not what you *think* you see." We will now apply this principle to an easy technique called "Attribute Listing," or "Morphological Analysis."

First, you take an object and just look at it. Next, you deconstruct it by listing its component parts one by one. List what you see, not what you *think* you see, as if you are seeing the object for the first time. Then you can list the uses of that product as part of the attributes and the assumptions behind the uses. You then play with your thoughts by coming up with alternatives for each one.

Here's an example: Let's say you are looking for ways ideas to improve the everyday product, the teacup. You list the attributes of that cup at the top of the following chart, listing the most mundane characteristics that seem rather obvious.

Cup	Handle	Saucer	Round	Holds Hot Liquid	Made of Porcelain

Now you generate a number of alternatives under each one in the columns. Notice that some of the alternatives below are "no handle" and "no saucer." Nothing is always an alternative to something and likewise, something to nothing.

	A. Cup	B. Handle	C. Saucer	D. Round	E. Holds Hot Liquids	F. Made of Porcelain
1.	Carton	No handle	Mini hot plate	Square	Holds breath mints	Made of rubber
2.	Glass with a pocket on the side	Lever on bottom of cup	Ring around top of cup to prevent spills	Triangular	Holds candies	Plastic
3.	Bottle	Finger indentations on cup sides	Saucer-shaped pastry	Spiraled	Holds both hot and cold liquids at same time	Glass
4.	Gel pack	Handle that folds into cup itself for stacking	No Saucer	Oval	Evaporates liquids	Recyclable paper
5.	Mini cups that fit together like puzzle pieces	Cup on wheels	Saucer shaped milk holder	Spiked	Solidifies liquids	Something edible

When you have generated multiple alternatives, from the mundane to the provocative, you are ready to mix and match them to see what ideas arise for a new teacup.

Take care not to go for the easiest combinations, though. The trick to this technique is to push yourself to entertain those unlikely combinations. One way to do this is to assign letters to the columns and numbers to the attribute, and then pick them randomly without looking at the table.

Let's say you chose A2, B5, C4, D1, E3 and F4. Combining these you would have a new design of a teacup in the shape of a drinking glass that sits on wheels instead of a saucer. It is square and has two compartments, one to hold tea, the other to hold the cinnamon stick or used teabag, and it is made from recyclable paper.

The more practice you get with this tool, the more you mix those combos that test your thinking. That is the five-star mindset of an innovator.

Chapter 12

The Mental Gymnastics of Provocation[80]

The exhilaration of skiing in deep powder is addictive. Out in the wilderness on a cold, sunny day, feeling the wind against your face, hearing only the swoosh of your skis as you glide on the soft powdery snow: this is what many skiers live for. It is a floating feeling that skiers often describe as dream-like. That was what Don had signed up for in a ski trip to Europe with friends, but what he experienced was a lot different. In fact, it was terrifying.

The trip to Cervinia, Italy, had been delayed by nearly a day because of the snow that had fallen for the previous 11 days. The bus from the airport had to make many unscheduled stops to wait for the roads to be cleared of snow. Reports of avalanches were constant, adding to the trepidation that Don tried to hide.

Now that they were finally standing at the top of the mountain, the long and arduous trip had been worth it. The sight of seven feet of virgin snow was surreal.

"You'll probably never see conditions like these again," said Mike, one of the guys on the trip. "Skiing in these conditions is a dream come true. See you at the gondola." Off he went.

Don and Jack watched Mike as he burst through the powdery snow like a thick cloud rolling down the slope. The Matterhorn glistened across the way, giving an effect that was almost spiritual.

80　A creative thinking technique first designed by E. de Bono. It is described in detail in *Serious Creativity*. New York: HarperCollins, 1993.

Don was barely an intermediate skier, and while he would not have admitted it, he was probably the least experienced in the group and more than a little nervous. But that wasn't going to stop him from enjoying this trip. In his mid-20s and emboldened by the naiveté that accompanies youth, he felt that the only way to get better was to just jump in and do it.

"Just lean back a bit on your skis and you'll be good to go," said his close buddy, Jack. "This is awesome!" Jack planted his poles and took off, barely visible as he flew downward in the powder that was around his shoulders. Don followed suit.

He felt the tension in his knees as he tried to maintain form and traversed a few times to slow his speed. It was very different from skiing on the hard-packed snow that he was used to, but he was beginning to understand why people raved about it.

The slope was steep, and Don could feel himself losing control as his speed increased, so he tried to traverse again. But this time, the powder seemed to get in the way between his legs, and he lost his balance. In an instant, he catapulted forward head first in the powder.

Falling was nothing new for Don, but falling in powder over his head was. He found himself disoriented, beneath a lot of lightly packed snow. Out of habit, he raised his head expecting to see the sky, but he was encased in the snow. He pulled his arms in and tried to pull his legs in too, but he felt stuck. One ski had come off; the other was on the end of his foot, jammed into the snow ahead of him. As he tried once more to pull his limbs inward, he realized that he did not know which way was up. It was the strangest feeling. As a relatively inexperienced skier, he also did not know that all he needed to do was spit, and that would tell him the direction of the ground.

He decided to lean forward and put his weight on the ski so he could step on it and pull himself up that way. As soon as he leaned into the ski, it moved further away in the snow. He tried again. It moved some more. In the numerous times he'd fallen before, he had taken for granted that simple move of standing up on a ski. Now there was no resistance. He didn't know what to do. Jack was probably halfway down the mountain by now, so he probably wasn't even aware of Don's plight.

Don started to sweat, because of both the physical effort of moving and the panic that was setting in. He stretched his legs out, hoping that he would feel the ground somewhere. Nothing. He reached forward to release his binding and free his other foot, holding onto his ski as if it were a life raft. He wondered: was this what it was like in an avalanche?

He felt very alone. He yelled, but he knew that his yell could not be heard through the snow that completely enveloped him. No sound came back. He struggled again, moving his arms and legs, as if flailing in slow motion. Every movement took effort.

After a time, Don, exhausted, was finally able to lift himself out of the snow by putting his foot back into his ski with less force. Once on the surface, he slowly slid forward and found his other ski. There was no one around. It was eerily quiet. Relieved and spent, he skied down the mountain, stopping frequently to avoid falling. It was a slow descent.

Don was more than a little shaken, and said nothing to his friends that evening. He did arrange to take some lessons in powder skiing later that week so that he would never find himself in that predicament again.

Disorientation causes discomfort, and the longer we experience this type of discomfort, the harder it is to withstand. We have a natural inclination to seek recognition of the familiar as quickly as possible so that we can get our bearings. As we saw in the previous examples of attempts to make sense of the world, when our thinking is disoriented, we naturally try to find answers by looking for patterns and connections to orient ourselves.

The normal person seldom feels disorientation while they are thinking. When it does occur, we feel usually feel it for a fleeting moment, like in a case of not knowing where you are while in a strange area, until you figure it out, if only in a general sense. If that lasts for more than a few seconds, it can elicit the same terrifying feeling as it did for Don.

This is the natural patterning system of the brain and is instrumental in our everyday functioning. If we had to analyze every detailed piece of information before acting, we would have a difficult time getting dressed in the morning. The benefit of this patterning is that we can be efficient, because we do not have to process every bit of information. We get the message without all the information because our patterning system fills in the blanks. We avoid the terrifying feeling of disorientation, but this efficiency can be detrimental to creative thinking, because it locks us into neural thinking patterns that inhibit us from forming new connections.

Every thought we have is connected to another thought. We do not think in a random fashion. This is why when we try brainstorming methods that do not break those patterns, the ideas end up being similar to one another. We are actually carrying the thread of the conversation throughout the brainstorm, which ends up being more of the same.

Provocation is a technique that de Bono developed to deliberately shock the mind out of existing ways of thinking. This technique deliberately disorients your thoughts so you are forced to consider nonsensical, disconnected ideas. Perhaps because it feels so uncomfortable, it is the most difficult type of creative thinking – but like the risk and reward principle, the more effort you put into it, the more original ideas you can yield.

DuPont has used this technique often and successfully. In looking for new uses for Lycra®, people at the company started with a statement that "Lycra® is used for stretch apparel, innerwear, women's wear, clothing for people, etc." They took something out of that and said "what about Lycra® for nonpersons?" That led to ideas for stretch clothing for dolls, stretch warm-up suits for racehorses and a host of accessory products related to these.[81]

Another successful idea came from DuPont's use of this tool when they were looking for ways to reduce costs in their information systems group. One of their managers, during a training session, came up with the phrase "Reduce costs by spending more money" to spark some creative thinking.[82] That led to the idea that spending more money on fewer vendors would result in greater volume discounts. This was counterintuitive to the prevailing thinking at the time, which was to have a large number of vendors who would compete against one another and therefore lower costs. This new direction led to savings of over $300,000 annually, and the DuPont employees then applied this concept to the maintenance department resulting in similar substantial savings.[83]

Plenty of examples of ideas have come from this type of creative thinking. "Holding a lottery with no raffle" led to self-administered lottery tickets, on which the purchaser scratches a piece of paper and the prize appears on it. "Calling before paying for a phone call" led to pre-paid calling cards. "Paying customers to buy something" led to the rebate concept. "A pencil that is never used up" led to the mechanical pencil with multiple lead pieces in refill cartridges.[84]

---

81 Tanner, D. *Total Creativity In Business & Industry*. Des Moines: Advanced Practical Thinking Training, Inc., 1997.
82 ibid, page 15
83 ibid.
84 Kotler, P. and Trias de Bes, F. *Lateral Marketing: New Techniques For Finding Breakthrough Ideas*. New Jersey: John Wiley & Sons, 2003.

An idea that revolutionized a whole industry came from the provocation "You die before you die."[85] Employees at Prudential were brainstorming ways to increase the revenues of their life insurance business. From this disorienting statement, the thinking evolved to what can you get before you die? Then it occurred to them that you could get a partial payout of your insurance to cover medical costs before you die. That led to the concept of Living Benefits. And as great ideas spawn other great ideas, it led to the concept of reverse mortgages where people who have paid for their homes can sell them back to the bank for a series of annuity payments. It is a convenient way for seniors to gain greater financial security to supplement their Social Security, and help people meet unexpected medical expenses, make home improvements and more. With the recent financial system collapse and stricter terms for lending, however, these ideas may not be as popular as they once were. But they were valuable at the time and a good illustration of how useful provocation can be.

Given the extreme cognitive manipulation inherent in the provocation technique, people either love it or hate it. For people who hate it, I can only say: stick with it and practice it, because it's worth the effort.

One group of senior team members of a financial services company in New York is glad that they did. They, like everyone else, had suffered significant losses in their investments and decided to use this technique to see if they could recoup some of their losses.

As a rule of thumb, investing in equities is usually a good strategy because if you pick the right companies to invest in, you will increase income from dividends and capital gains as the stock value rises. But given the market, the statement that truthfully described the equity

---

85   de Bono, E. (ibid.)

market was "Equities are bad investments." The team members turned that into what was at the time an untruthful statement, "Equities are good investments," and then used that as its perceptual filter to look at companies to invest in. It was exactly the opposite of what they would normally do in that investment market.

They targeted companies with earnings that were severely compromised, enough to qualify them for government bailout money, in an attempt to stave off bankruptcy. In conducting their due diligence, they uncovered some impressive investment strategies that differentiated the high- and low-performing portfolios within one particular company division. It was akin to finding a diamond in the rough. They bought that division at one-third less than original price paid for it by the parent company and added earnings-per-share to their own company the following year at a time when many companies in the industry were faltering.

People react differently to getting lost, whether it is on vacation or in thought. Some become impatient and feel their time is being wasted as they try to find their bearings. Others remain relaxed and take the situation in stride. They might even view the occasion as an adventure, because they get to meander through the streets absorbing new sights and sounds, unaffected by the pressures of time.

It takes patience to let your mind ponder illogical thoughts. The best approach to provocation is to relax into it, ponder each thought and just see where it takes you. It is simply part of the journey. The sooner you do that, the sooner provocation will become part of your successful creative thinking repertoire.

One of the best kids' birthday parties ever was a backwards party. The invitations were printed so they could be read only with a mirror. The attendees were invited to come to the back door, dressed backwards. The rest of it went as you might expect: the kids came in summer clothes for a winter party. Some of them wore clothes inside-out. Others wore pajamas. Presents were wrapped with the colored part of the wrapping paper inside. When they arrived at the door, the hostess cried "Goodbye!"

The kids played Silent Chairs, and they made inside-out piñatas by taking balloons with their names written on them (backwards, of course). When the hostess dumped bags of penny candy on the floor, the kids raced to tape candy onto the outside of their piñatas. Everything was inside-out and backwards. Now think of this as you practice Provocation as a thinking technique. It can be fun if you let it be!

A similar creative thinking technique is SCAMPER developed by Bob Eberle.[86] It is an acronym that stands for:

S - Substitute - materials, people, parts

C - Combine – mix or combine

A - Adapt - alter, change function, or use part of it

M - Modify - increase or reduce in size, change shape, modify attributes

P - Put to another use – find another way to use the product or service

E - Eliminate - remove elements, simplify, take something out

R - Reverse - turn inside out or upside down.

---

86   Eberle, R. (1996). SCAMPER: *Creative Games and Activities for Imagination Development.* USA: Prufrock Press.

It is an effective technique to modify a product or service, or create an entirely new one.

Here's how you might use it. Say, for example, that you're looking for new ideas to improve the suitcase. Here's how it could be applied:

S - Substitute - Instead of the traditional canvas or leather, make it out of a durable plastic that you could post your favorite pictures in, changing them from time to time

C - Combine – Instead of having a separate bag or purse with your travel documents, plane munchies and reading materials inside, combine it with the suitcase itself so that it attaches to the outside. When you are about to store it in the overhead or check it, just pull off the outer mini-bag where you have everything you need for the plane in one piece.

A - Adapt - alter, change function, or use part of it. Alter the suitcase so that when it is empty, you can collapse the side folds in on each other making it a flat structure on wheels, similar to a dolly. You can then use it to pull heavy items when you're walking or traveling by foot locally.

M - Modify - increase or reduce in size, change shape, modify attributes. Make the suitcase in modular pieces so that you can have two or three self-contained parts that fit together. That way you can use the whole thing when you need to or only a small part of it when you need less. It then becomes not just a suitcase, but a briefcase or carry-all.

P - Put to another Use – a suitcase that can transform into a set of roller skates or something that the traveler can wear to get from one place to another quickly

E - Eliminate - remove elements, simplify, take something out. Remove all zipper pull tags so that every tag is recessed. This way they won't break off with rough use during their handling in transit.

R - Reverse - turn inside out or upside down. Design a suitcase that will never be upside down because it is shaped round like a wheel. It can then travel over many different types of surfaces more easily. (It turns out that there is such a bag - the Samsonite OBAG designed by Rooz Mousavi) [87]

Now see what you can do with this technique. First, think of what you want to get some ideas on and write it down.

What do I want to get ideas for?

_____

_____

Now apply each of the following:

Substitute	
Combine	
Adapt	
Modify	
Put to New Use	
Eliminate	
Reverse	

87   Rolling Bag, Literally. *Yanko Design*. Retrieved August 5, 2010 from http://www. yankodesign.com/ 2008/09/22/rolling-bag-literally

Chapter 13

Going Green: Servicizing vs. Ownership

"The only reason a great many American families
don't own an elephant is that they have
never been offered an elephant for a dollar
down and easy weekly payments." [88]

A generation ago, closets in homes were small openings that barely contained a few articles of clothing on hangers. Now, they are walk-ins, about as large as master bedrooms. These closets are a testament to the fact that we have lots and lots of stuff – too much stuff, some would say. Consumerism and materialism have become rampant to the point where we are starting to see reverse trends like voluntary simplicity, a movement where a growing number of people are reducing their personal possessions in favor of simplicity.

Dr. Mary Grigsby, an associate professor of rural sociology at the University of Missouri, in Columbia, says, "The idea in the voluntary simplicity movement was 'everything you own, owns you.' You have to care for it, store it. It becomes an appendage – If it enhances your life and helps you do the things you want to do, great. If you are burdened by these things and they become the center of what you have to do to live, is that really positive?"[89]

---

88 Golbguru. An Elephant For A Dollar Down And Easy Weekly Payments. August 6, 2007. In *Money, Matter, and More Musings* Musings on Money, Personal Finance, Frugality, Debt, and Other Matters

89 Grigbsy M. (2004). Buying Time and Getting by: *The Voluntary Simplicity Movement.* New York: SUNY Press

This line of thought has a common-sense ring to it, but having what we want instead of wanting what we have still appears to be the norm, and our society is built around it. In fact, the gross domestic product ("GDP"), which is the level of economic activity achieved, is regarded as a measure of a nation's progress. More is believed to be ipso facto better bolstering the "have-more" ethos of our society.

Economic progress can still be a laudable goal so long as it is not an end in itself.

In 1989, Alaska's G.D.P. rose when local hotels, restaurants, stores and gas stations all experienced an increase in business, but it was hardly progress. The increase came because so many people were involved in the cleaning up of the Exxon Valdez oil spill. Of course, markets are supposed to be efficient, not necessarily fair.

The fact is that shopping had become a pastime for many. While it has slowed because of the economic downturn, it will likely return to pre-recession levels unless those people adopt a drastically different, more eco-effective mindset. Also, it's easier to throw away something than to get it repaired. By some estimates, more than 90 percent of materials extracted to make durable goods in the U.S. become waste right away.[90] Think about the last time you bought a sandwich for lunch or a candy bar. Most likely you threw away the wrapping in the trash before taking a bite. While writing this book, I changed the print cartridge on my printer and had to throw away a heavy, plastic cartridge container that was three times the size of the cartridge. (As my printer is near the end of its life cycle, I plan on changing it soon to one that uses cartridges in less packaging.)

---

90   McDonough, W. and Braungart, M. (2002). *Cradle to Cradle*. New York: North Point Press.

Landfills are full of furniture, carpets, clothing, telephones, packaging, diapers, you name it. Population growth is increasing on this finite planet Earth, and it's becoming painfully clear that we cannot throw things away any more, because there is no "away." The slogan "reduce, reuse and recycle" was a good start on addressing this issue, but now we have to up the ante and think of our planet as the closed loop system it is, and eliminate waste.

Enter the innovative concept of "servicizing."[91] Instead of selling a product to produce an end result, sell the result itself, directly and efficiently, without the peripheral or supportive elements. In other words, if you want to be cooled on a hot summer day, buy the air without the air conditioner. Why bother with the maintenance, winterizing and cleaning? This represents a shift in the business paradigm: manufacturers go from selling ownership of a product to selling leases.

Carrier, a market leader in air-conditioning equipment and a pioneer in this concept, now offers "coolth" services, by which the customer leases an air conditioner, getting the cool air, while Carrier looks after the maintenance. By challenging the concept of the "product" it was selling, Carrier achieved another benefit. The company is no longer just conducting a transaction; rather, it is improving its relationship with the customer.

This change in thinking didn't end there because it still needed to replace some of the revenues it made on the sales of the unit. So now Carrier has partnerships with other companies to provide windows, retrofit lighting and upgrade buildings to get efficient temperature control, without waste, in both warmth and coolth.

---

91   Stahel, W. and Braungart, M. in Hawken, P., Lovins, A. and Hunter-Lovins, L. (1999). *Natural Capitalism*. New York: Little Brown and Co.

At first glance, it might seem counterintuitive that Carrier makes more money when it sells less of its product. But in re-defining its product, it opens up other areas to add value and charge for it. The less equipment Carrier has to provide to deliver comfort, the more money it makes.

Another advantage of this arrangement is that the customer and supplier no longer have opposing interests. In the traditional buy-sell arrangement, the customer wants to buy the most at the lowest cost, while the seller wants to give the least for the highest cost. In the new model, both make money in the same way and increase resource productivity in the meantime[92].

Servicizing made inroads in the car industry back in the 1990s. Ford recognized that a significant amount of the paint it was buying did not end up on vehicles because of inefficient manufacturing processes.[93] Much of the paint was escaping as air emissions or water-based sludge. So DuPont and Ford renegotiated their relationship; now, rather than selling paint to Ford, DuPont sells a service of painted cars. This gives DuPont an incentive to paint cars with the least amount of waste, resulting in savings for both companies and increased efficiencies.

A more recent example of servicizing in the auto industry is the trend to car sharing. The Zipcar and Flexcar, in New York City, represent this new concept. You can rent a car when you need it, even if for only an hour, for as little as $8 per hour. As Zipcar says in it's advertising, "It's like having your own car in the city, but with free gas and insurance."[94] Apparently over 40 percent of these car sharers end up selling their cars or decide not to buy one. Car usage is reduced by as much as 50 percent,

---

92 Hawken, P., Lovins, A. and Hunter-Lovins, L. (1999). *Natural Capitalism*. New York: Little Brown and Co.

93 http://www.rand.org/scitech/stpi/ourfuture/Consumer/sec6_marketplace.html

94 Zipcar. Wheels when you want them. Retrieved http://www.zipcar.com/webny.

and Zipcar members use the most efficient means of transportation, be it walking, biking, public transportation, taxi or Zipcar.

The benefits of this, of course, are legion. Each car replaces 15 privately owned cars in an urban area, which means less road congestion, less gas consumption, fewer fuel emissions and more green space, because fewer parking spaces are needed.[95]

On a trip to Frankfurt, Germany, I discovered a similar innovative idea with bike sharing. Most street corners had a handful of bikes available for rent. There was a number to call to get the lock code in exchange for a credit card payment. I took a bike, rode it for a couple of hours, then returned it in another area of the city. I placed one more call to the company so they could track the time I had it. It couldn't have been easier.

Taking this concept further, a carpet sales company in Atlanta called Interface Flooring turned itself into a carpet-leasing agent. Company officials figured that the customer wants what the carpet offers, not what it is. So now, cushioning on the floor for style, noise reduction and comfort can be had without owning it. The company supplies carpet tiles; worn pieces in the high traffic areas can be replaced and recycled. The company has an incentive, then, to make the carpet as durable as possible, saving energy and natural resources, and reducing landfill waste.[96]

The chemical industry is following suit. Many solvents are toxic and flammable, and the consumer has the responsibility of disposing of them safely. Dow Chemical Company and SafetyKleen will lease the solvents. Their employees deliver the solvent, help the customer apply it and then take it away. The customer is no longer responsible for the disposal.

---

95 Car Sharing: Where and How it Succeeds. *TCRP Report* 108. Retrieved from http:// books. google.com/books?.

96 Benyus, J. *Biomimicry : Innovation Inspired by Nature,* William Morrow & Co.: New York: 2002

The tech industry sets another good example. Questioning the norm, Sun Microsystems shifted away from the current model in which every employee has a desktop or a laptop computer. Instead, they use a system in which files, applications and settings are stored on efficient, shared servers and accessed by logging into network-enabled terminals.[97] Sun calls it the "Desktop over IP" or "thin client" model. In the larger world of information technology, this practice is known as "cloud computing" – common business applications are provided online and can be accessed from a Web browser via a BlackBerry or iPhone with the software and data stored on the servers.

As with any new concept or idea, servicizing has drawbacks. The business partners will develop greater interdependencies with the ongoing relationship. When the product ages and inefficiencies begin to occur, or the product breaks down and causes delays or quality problems, these relationships can be strained. In practical terms, something like quality, for example, is often hard to measure; certain issues will have to be clearly set out in contracts to guard against liability risks. The tax treatment of ownership is still more favorable than of leasing and will need to be amended. Yet in many areas, it would seem that the benefits of servicizing outweigh the disadvantages, especially when considering the impact on the environment.

Innovators see this as an opportunity to apply this concept elsewhere. Focusing on mundane products can be a fun thought experiment.

Take detergent for washing clothes. What exactly does the consumer want? The soap. What can be cut? The container. How can you provide soap as a service? This opens up new possibilities as you move away from one-size-fits-all soap packaging. Perhaps you can sell soap by weight.

---

97   Westervelt, A. Service me. Sustainable Industries. Sustainable Media Inc. June 6, 2007

Water quality differs by region. In areas of soft water, relatively small amounts of detergent are needed; in areas with hard water, larger amounts are needed. The economy of scale achieved through mass production of same-size products could be replaced by customized product sizes to fit each market. Manufacturers would then have to weigh the cost of this approach against the benefit of less waste and environmental pollution.

Given the rising importance of environmental concerns, it seems unlikely that servicizing will go away. Corporations may well find it in their best interests to re-define the costs of environmental degradation by taking into account the greater costs of expanding landfills on a finite earth. It took innovation to conceive of mass manufacturing methods, and it will be through continuous innovations that we will make servicizing work while still achieving profitability.

This nascent trend is not only gaining popularity in businesses, but may also soon see regulation. The U.S. government now has an environmental most-wanted list for people who are accused of environmental crimes.[98] They are fugitives who allegedly dumped hazardous waste into rivers and oceans, dumped oil or smuggled chemicals that harm the ozone layer. Their profiles and pictures are now listed on an Environmental Protection Agency Web site, http://www.epa.gov/fugitives, asking for help in providing information leading to any arrests.

---

98   Criminal Enforcement. EPA Fugitives. Retrieved May 15, 2009 from http://www.epa.gov/fugitives.

Exercise: Think Service, Not Product

Think about how you can turn these products into services. Remember that all ideas are good ideas, even if they do not appear to be. If you don't like one, just use it as a seed or stepping stone to further thoughts. Recall, too, that many provocative ideas are not cost effective. In fact, they are often cost prohibitive. Entertain the idea or concept without concern for the cost. That way, you will not prematurely filter your thinking process.

Product	Peripherals of Product You Can Eliminate	Servicizing Concept
Pet food	Food containers, dirty dishes, leftover food bits	Deliver meals to pets and take away dishes
Warm Outer Clothing	Winter Coat	A rental kiosk where travelers can rent winter coats at airports when traveling from a warm climate to a cold one
Bottled Water	Plastic bottle	Set up water stations in neighborhoods where you can deliver other services such as car washes at people's homes
Rain Protection	Umbrella	???
Suntan lotion	Lotion	???

Reflection:

In order to adopt an eco-innovator's mindset, every time you pick up a product, whether it is something as mundane as a container of juice or a computer printer, let your mind wander and ask yourself how you could provide that same product without the peripheral contents.

Chapter 14

Silence is Golden

An old Egyptian proverb says, "Silence is more profitable than abundance of speech." Yet in our busy world with piped-in music, iPods, pagers and the endless cell phone abusers inflicting their conversations on everyone around them, silence has become elusive. To get the most of your thinking, you must bring back the silence, even in a group brainstorming session.

People normally prefer group sessions because they generate more energy, but the drawback is that they can limit an individual's thinking. Participants offer their ideas orally, often times in a free-for-all fashion. But there are problems with this practice.

First, the extroverts usually share their ideas first, because they are more comfortable among other people, and they end up drowning out the quieter group members, who have just as much to share. Second, if one person offers an impressive idea, another may choose not to share hers because she feels hers to be inferior, when, in fact, it may have much merit. Third, people, for various reasons, think in different ways and at different speeds. The time of day may determine their level of alertness. Some people take time to delve deeply into a thought; others think more fluidly, jumping quickly from one thought to another. Both are valuable, but those who need more time to finish their thoughts may be in the midst of formulating an idea or concept in their mind, but others' speech takes them off their thought track and the idea is lost.

For these reasons, I highly recommend a minute or two of thinking in silence before the group discussion. You will get a greater number of ideas to start the session off, and therefore more ideas upon which to build.

One way to do this is the BOAT technique, "Building On Another's Thoughts." No more than five or six people participate. Everyone gets a sheet of paper and writes the focus or target of their thinking as follows.

Focus: New Ways to Improve Customer Relationships

	Round One	Round Two	Round Three
Idea # 1			
Idea # 2			
Idea # 3			
Idea # 4			

Each round consists of three to four minutes. In Round 1, each person writes four ideas in the column as succinctly as possible. Then the facilitator calls the time, and each person passes his or her worksheet to the person on the right. In Round 2, participants build upon or modify the ideas described. If they come up with entirely new ideas, they write those down too. In three to four minutes, a new round begins. At the end of the rounds, you can easily yield a hundred ideas for potential further development.

To make the most of both individual and group thinking, this technique is best followed by a group session to take advantage of the higher energy. The group can work further on the ideas they think are the best, using the techniques mentioned earlier.

Part Three

Chapter 15

Innovation for the Greater Good

In the late 1980s, Dean Kamen, a college dropout and self-taught entrepreneur, watched a man in a wheelchair struggling to get up on a curb. He wondered whether he could build a chair that would hop curbs without losing its balance.

Never daunted by a challenge, he set to work and didn't stop until he had something. It was not the first time he had designed a product that would make a difference in people's lives, and it probably won't be the last. (Kamen holds 440 U.S. and foreign patents, many of them for innovative medical devices that have significantly improved health care around the world.)[99]

This time Kamen, in partnership with Johnson and Johnson's Independence Technology division, invented the iBot™, a mobility system that functions as an automated wheelchair and much more. It can climb stairs, cross curbs and traverse rocks and even sand. It is a system with sensors and gyroscopes that send information to software, allowing it to not only have a sense of balance, but also raise the user to others' eye levels.[100]

Kamen's other inventions include the Autosyringe, a device that delivers medicine automatically, which led to the development of the insulin pump that is now worn by millions of diabetics. He invented a dialysis machine the size of a phone book in the mid-1990s, when dialysis

---

99   Deka. Evolved thinkers. Retrieved from http://www.dekaresearch.com/founder.shtml.
100   Information for iBot owners. Retrieved January 20, 2009 from http://www.ibotnow.com/functions/mobility-system.html.

machines were large and bulky, and patients could use them only in hospitals.

One of his latest inventions is the Segway Human Transporter, a two-wheeled, self-balancing electric vehicle, whose users need only lean forward or backward to move in a given direction.

These are but a few of his inventions that significantly improve the lives of others. To encourage innovation, Kamen also operates a nonprofit venture called U.S. First (For Inspiration and Recognition of Science and Technology), which encourages children and teens to follow careers in engineering or science.

We need more people like Kamen who innovate for the greater good, just as we need more people who simply reach out because they want to help in their own small way.

Thirteen years ago, Betsy and Jared Saul, then a young, married couple of cash poor graduate students in New Jersey, were discussing ways to design the perfect Web site. Back then, in 1996, Web site development was in its early phases. It was a "what if" type of discussion, because they had both just finished their degrees and were about to embark on careers in medicine and groundwater hydrology.

If they had the perfect Web site, they mused, where would it best be used? For a good cause, they agreed, and one that could not afford advertising or marketing. They decided on animal shelters. Although both were busy, they felt that they had an ethical obligation to move forward, and that if they could "save just one pet a month, it would be worth it."[101] With the help of family and friends, they built Petfinder.com. Now 1.5 million pets a year find homes thanks to this couple reaching out to serve the greater good.

---

101 Abern, A. (2009) Marley & Gina & Me. *Best Friends Magazine*, January/February 2009.

Businesses exist for many reasons. Even though not every business can contribute directly to the greater good, enterprises can do so indirectly without significantly compromising profits. Now, as we experience the disastrous effects of runaway growth, there is a growing realization that it is not enough to stay in business and be profitable.

With the collapse of companies built on greed in an era of making money from money without adding true value to society, society now seems to be suggesting that big corporations like General Electric, and Nike should re-invest at least some of their profits to the benefit of all. That implies a greater need for authentic and integral business leadership in building lasting and sustained value in serving not just customers and staff members, but also humanity. In effect, what we are seeing is a renewed focus on building more social capitalism[102] to encourage positive and healthy development for society in general.

In 2005, General Electric CEO Jeffery Immelt launched a business strategy that focuses on a green initiative. He called it Ecomagination and its primary objective is to create environmental solutions to produce cleaner water and energy. It is a prime example of building social capitalism. Displayed on the GE Web site are the words: Innovation = Imagination, stating that the company is determined to solve the world's biggest problems, one idea at a time.

Nike, who once had been hurt over the discovery of its sweatshops overseas, has now instituted its own brand of social capitalism in its "Considered" program. They claim to be making improvements in reducing greenhouse gases and making cleaner, more sustainable designs where their overseas employees no longer have to handle toxic chemicals and wear facial masks.

---

102 Social capitalism, challenges the idea that socialism and capitalism are inherently antagonistic. It is seen as the ability for a company to have or create positive, healthy development.

Making eco-sustainability and social capitalism the guideposts for creative thinking can be intrinsically rewarding work for the socially conscious. The realization that our planet is a closed loop system that consists of interdependent elements is increasingly permeating the social consciousness. Innovating with the notion that we all live downwind of each other will help us stay on the right track.

Measuring the details of environmental impact on consumer products by counting the greenhouse gases produced in making, transporting and selling them is an encouraging new trend in this direction.[103] The footwear manufacturer Timberland now has a label that details the energy used in making the shoes, the portion that is renewable, and the factory's labor record -- although assessing the exact environmental costs may be more of an art than a science because you'd have to measure back to the cow that supplied the leather.

Some feel that this labeling needs to be more stringent, for example with an independent evaluation rather than one conducted by the companies themselves. The nonprofit group Climate Counts, funded by Stonyfield Farm, is one such company that will independently evaluate consumer-products companies' efforts to manage their effects on the environment, although the funding by Stonyfield Farm calls into question its 'independence'. The idea is to create a system that will let consumers compare the carbon footprints of companies like McDonalds and Burger King so a consumer can choose which is better on the environment. One day there may be a standard electronic form of labeling where consumers will be able to point cell phones at interactive electronic tags on products to get more information than could ever fit on a printed label.[104]

---

103 Cortese, A. "Friend of Nature? Let's see those shoes." *New York Times*.
Retrieved from http://www.nytimes.com/ 2007/03/07/business/businessspecial2/07label-sub.html.

OUR FOOTPRINT   *NOTRE EMPREINTE*

Climate Impact[1]   *Incidences sur le climat[1]*

Use of renewable energy
Utilisation d'énergie renouvelable   6.36%

Chemicals Used[2]   *Produits chimiques utilisés[2]*

PVC-free   *Sans PVC*   81.14%

Resource Consumption   *Consommation de ressources*

Eco-conscious materials[3]
Matériaux écologiques[3]   5.27%

Recycled content of shoebox
*Contenu en matières recyclées de la boîte de
chaussures*   100%

Trees planted through 2007
Nombre d'arbres plantés en 2007   668,225

*For more information visit www.timberland.com/footprint
Pour plus d'information : www. timberland.com/footprint*

[1] *Measured against approximately 14% of Timberland's total
climate impact for 2008. (excludes, e.g., licensees and third
party factories).
Mesuré contre 14% environ de l'impact de climat total de Timberland pour le compte de l'année 2008. (À l'exclusion, par exemple,
des détenteurs de permis et des usines de tierces parties)*

[2] *Footwear skus produced in 2007. Measure excludes trace elements.
Modèles de chaussures fabriqués en 2007. La mesure exclut
les oligo-éléments.*

[3] *Footwear skus produced in 2007 with at least 10% recycled,
renewable and/or organic materials in one or more components.
Look for the eco-conscious icons.
Modèles de chaussures fabriqués en 2007 contenant au moins
10 % de matériau recyclé, renouvelable ou organique, dans
une ou plusieurs parties de la chaussure. Recherchez les
symboles écologiques.*

*Timberland footwear includes: Timberland and non-licensed
Timberland PRO.
Les chaussures Timberland comprennent : Timberland et
Timberland PRO.*

*Printed on 100% post consumer recycled material.
Imprimé sur matériau recyclé post-consommation à 100 %.*

Permission to reproduce from Cara Vanderbeck, of Timberland, March 5, 2009.

Product certifications for eco-sustainability are a natural outgrowth of this measuring trend. The Cradle to Cradle™ Product Certification by McDonough Braungart Design Chemistry is one such program founded by William McDonough, an architect, and Michael Braungart a chemist, in 1955. They evaluate human and environmental health impacts throughout a product's lifecycle, as well as assessing the product's potential for being truly recycled or safely composted. That includes the evaluation of energy and water use, water-effluent quality, and workplace ethics associated with manufacturing.

One of the first certifications is the Steelcase's Think® chair, which can be disassembled with ordinary hand tools in about five minutes. Human and environmental health are considered in the manufacturing of the chair to the extent that the origin of the chair's materials, the way it is made, and what it will be when it is no longer a chair are important factors for certification. The result is a chair that is up to 98% recyclable by weight, using up to 37% recycled content.

The impetus to innovate with a green focus can only become stronger, as we see more and more carbon caps instituted and the emergence of more eco-sustainability regulations. This trend does not guarantee improving the greater good directly, but working in consonance with the environment will help us avoid the harm we have inflicted until now. Fortunately, efforts to helping others directly are positively reinforced because the desire to help is a powerful, intrinsic motivator. That is an absolute necessity to stay the course, because turning an innovation into a success almost always requires overcoming significant resistance.

---

104 ibid.

Chapter 16

Getting Past Resistance

The German philosopher Arthur Schopenhauer once said that
all truth goes through three phases. First, it is ridiculed. Second, it is
violently opposed. Third, it is accepted as being self-evident. It is an apt
description of what often happens when an innovative idea or concept is
first introduced. Judah Folkman experienced this first-hand.[105]

Folkman was a U.S. Navy doctor in the 1960s who spent many
months at sea on aircraft carriers. His job was to find a way to preserve
fresh blood for use in surgery.

He experimented to see if he could design a system that could handle
fast growing cells, such as those that occur during the healing process.
After injecting cancer cells into rabbit thyroid cells, in vitro, and into
live mice, he found that the cells developed into deadly tumors in the
mice, but not so much in the in vitro thyroid cells. They developed into
tumors, but the tumors were very small and relatively harmless.

What accounted for this difference, he believed, was that the
tumor cells in the live mice were in contact with blood vessels, and that
cancerous tumors need blood to grow. Capillaries, or tiny blood vessels,
transport oxygen and nutrients to cells in the body and they export waste.
Tumors need capillaries to survive. This was a novel hypothesis; in 1971,
he published it in the New England Journal of Medicine.

Folkman was labeled a charlatan even though he was a Harvard
Medical professor and head of surgery at Children's Hospital.[106] The
problem was that he could not explain how the tumors took control

---

105 Servan-Schriber, David (2008). *Anti-Cancer: A New Way of Life*. London: Viking Penguin.
106 ibid.

of the blood vessels. He was ridiculed by colleagues and snubbed at conferences. Even his students started to avoid him, and he eventually lost his position as head of surgery.

For nearly 20 years he was scorned, but he never stopped seeking the answer.

Finally, a young researcher named Michael O'Reilly joined his lab, and found a protein that blocked the production of blood vessels.[107] It was the mechanism Folkman had been looking for all those years.

Angiogenesis, from the Greek words *angio* for vessel and *genesis* for birth, is what Folkman had labeled the process. Today, it is regarded as one of the major breakthroughs in cancer treatment.

I share this story with you because it shows the importance of persistence, self-confidence and unwavering belief in success against strong odds. As you have seen, some innovations are the result of serendipity and happenstance, but many occur only when a champion doggedly persists. There are, no doubt, countless others who would not have stayed the course in the face of such scorn all those years.

Often when we hear stories of inventions and breakthroughs, we are hearing the shortened version of history. Few innovations are instant successes.

Chris Haney and Scott Abbot know this only too well. They were two Canadian friends who used to play Scrabble a lot. They played so much, in fact, that when they went to replace the pieces missing from Chris's game, they realized that it was their sixth Scrabble set. It was then that they decided to invent a game of their own.

Both were avid trivia buffs. Within a few hours on that day in 1979, they invented a board game that Time magazine later called the "the

---

107 O'Reilly, M.S., L. Holmgren, Y. Shing, et al., "Angiostatin: A Novel Angiogenesis Inhibitor That Mediates the Suppression of Metastases by a Lewis Lung Carcinoma" Cell 79, no. 2 (1994): 315-328

biggest phenomenon in game history."[108] Two years later, they registered the trademark for Trivial Pursuit, and in March 2008, Hasbro Inc. purchased Trivial Pursuit for $80 million.[109]

That is the short story. These entrepreneurs worked at day jobs while they pursued the game.

Chris was a photo editor for The Montreal Gazette and Scott a sportswriter for The Canadian Press. It took both of them five months of 16-hour days to write the questions. They borrowed money from family and friends and had to learn how to market and sell their game. Making the actual games was expensive, and it wasn't long before they had exhausted their savings and Chris had driven himself to anxiety attacks. They were refused a loan and felt that they had hit the bottom.

It was only through persistence and determination that they continued to make ends meet. Chris's wife got a part-time nursing job to help with the bills, and Scott's father gave them a loan. Word of mouth about the game spread, and eventually things turned around.

Barbie is another example of a challenge that required a lot of patience and dogged persistence. The co-founder of Mattel, Ruth Handler, knew from her own experience in watching her daughter, Barbara, that little girls want to be like mommies when they play. The project their wishes and future visions onto the dolls, yet there were very few adult dolls on the market. Instead, most dolls were babies. None of those adult dolls had affordable, grown-up accessories.[110]

108 Bellis, M. The History of Trivial Pursuit." Retrieved May 13, 2009 from http://inventors. about.com/library/ inventors/trivia_pursuit.htm.

109 Cassie Tweten, (2008). History of Trivial Pursuit Board Game: The Story of Chris Haney and Scott Abbot's Popular Game Invention. Retrieved from Website://hobbies.suite101.com/ article.cfm/trivial_pursuit.

110 http://www.crazyforbarbie.com/barbiedollhistory.php

She shared this insight with her co-founder and some other toy designers, but received a cool reception. They couldn't see what she saw, a common reaction to innovative ideas.

A few years later, while traveling in Europe, she came across a doll with adult characteristics modeled after a character in a German comic strip. She brought three of them home to show the company directors. Finally, they saw the potential, and it was then that the challenges began.

The Barbie design required new manufacturing techniques, and the company undertook an exhaustive search that led them to a manufacturer in Japan.

More problems surfaced. The hair was difficult to attach. The fabrics had to be specially designed, and it was a challenge to manufacture something that was soft enough for children to play with, but hard enough to withstand child's play. It took about three years and many new processes to finally make it. Then another set of problems arose.

Finally, Barbie was introduced to the marketplace, and her mature body horrified many of the mothers.[111] Women found the sexy clothing disgusting, and the company faced the very real possibility that it would have a huge unsold inventory in Japan. But company officials continued, believing that young girls would go for Barbie, and marketing efforts were targeted to those girls.

It was the post-war era, and the economy was strong. Children had their own money and didn't have to rely on their parents. The toy industry did not respond well, but the young girls did. Barbie became not only a blockbuster, but also a huge cultural phenomenon. Mattel now grosses over $1 billion a year from Barbie and its related sales.

---

111 Wolf, Erica. Barbie. "The Early History." *The Beat Begins: America in the 1950s*. 2000. Retrieved May 16, 2009 from http://www.honors.umd.edu/HONR269J/projects/wolf.html.

Corporate innovations can sometimes be just as difficult even when financial issues are of no concern. This was the case with Proctor & Gamble, the maker of Crest toothpaste.

Dental disease had become a big health concern in the United States at the beginning of World War II. Scientists knew that cavities were caused by carbohydrates in food that were converted to acids by enzymes produced by bacteria in the mouth, but methods to treat them and improve oral health were a mixed bag. No one really knew if it was better to kill the bacteria or the enzymes.

Around that time, the U.S. Public Health Service did uncover an interesting fact: They found that children in some communities out West did not get cavities, and closer scrutiny revealed that their water contained natural fluoride. So scientists at P&G ran tests to duplicate these results and did, indeed, confirm this correlation. They then searched for a way to put fluoride in toothpaste, but found that the abrasives in toothpaste were incompatible with it. They tested over 500 different fluoride compounds before they were able to include one that worked.

Clinical trials were done with nearly 6,000 schoolchildren and the results were encouraging. The American Dental Association (ADA), however, did not endorse the idea, saying that it was not aware of any adequate evidence that demonstrated the claimed value of Crest. Another problem was that consumers were skeptical of the benefits because they did not know what fluoride was and what it could do. Proving the benefits meant that consumers would have to wait a year or two before they could compare. It would take approximately that long to show whether cavities would form or not.

In need of an endorsement, P&G submitted its test results to the ADA. It was a risk because the ADA had never before formally recognized any toothpaste.[112] It took five years for the ADA to review the toothpaste, and they finally endorsed it, granting the use of its name in consumer advertising for a commercial product for the first time.

During those five years, P&G did a lot of groundwork to get other endorsements, sending teams of people around the country to educate dentists about the product. It was only then that sales doubled, then tripled, and Crest became the best-selling toothpaste in the United States.

Innovations often meet resistance, whether it is in the form of ridicule, money, uneducated consumers, an undeveloped market or a lack of perceived need or value.

Einstein could not get a job when he finished university, and for a long while believed that he was useless. Buckminster Fuller was known as a crackpot for most of his life. When the Wright brothers took their first flight, the audience was small because their act was not regarded as a big event.

Consider these comments in response to some well-known innovations[113]:

"Well-informed people know it is impossible to transmit the voice over wires and that were it possible to do so, the thing would be of no practical value."

Editorial in The Boston Post, 1865

---

112 Strauss, S. (2002). Chicago: Dearborn Trade Publishing.
113 An excerpt from Time Magazine, Vol.83 no.2, January 10, 1964.

"I think I may say without contradiction that when the Paris Exhibition closes, electric light will close with it, and no more will be heard of it."

Erasmus Wilson, professor at Oxford University, 1878

"There will never be a mass market for motor cars -- about 1,000 in Europe -- because that is the limit on the number of chauffeurs available!"

Spokesman for Daimler Benz

"The average American family hasn't time for television."

The New York Times, 1939

"I think there is a world market for maybe five computers."

Thomas Watson, Chairman, IBM, 1949

"Man will never reach the moon regardless of all future scientific advances."

Dr. Lee De Forest (inventor of the vacuum tube), 1957

"The world potential market for copying machines is 5,000 at most."

IBM to the founders of Xerox, 1959

Clearly, anything that challenges our current belief system will not be accepted without some degree of difficulty. Making innovation happen often takes political skill and business savvy, as well as perseverance and belief. And sometimes it just takes time for people to appreciate the innovation or see the merit in it.

Chapter 17

Give Yourself the Gift of Time

Thomas Edison was regarded as quite a workaholic. He slept only five hours a night. And although he spent many long days in his lab, he also spent a good deal of his time alone, fishing. But oddly, he never caught any fish. It wasn't because he lacked the skills to fish. It was because he fished without any bait. Then why, colleagues asked, would he bother to go fishing? "Because," he said, "people don't bother you and neither do the fish. It provides me my best time to think."[114]

That precious, finite commodity of time, as Edison and others have recognized, is a key factor in enriching your thinking. Many of us, at one time to another, have lamented, "I just don't have time to think." Undoubtedly, the creative thinking techniques in this book provide a toolkit of options you can use without having to carve out an inordinate amount of time. But that does not mean that your time to reflect should be sacrificed. Creativity is a process, not a program. Bolstering innovation in companies requires a process that is a holistic system that permeates all layers. But often, the problem is that employees are overloaded with work and do not have that luxury of time to think.

Theresa Amabile, a Harvard Business School professor who has studied creativity extensively, found in research that very high levels of time pressure should be avoided if you want to foster creativity on a consistent basis. But, paradoxically, participants in a 10-year study gave

---

114 Newton, James D. (1987). *Uncommon Friends: Life With Thomas Edison, Henry Ford, Harvey Firestone, Alexis Carrel, & Charles Lindbergh.* Florida: Harcourt Publishers.

evidence of less creative thinking on time-pressured days, yet reported feeling more creative on those days.[115]

What is it about unpressured time that fosters creativity? Simply measuring the relationship of time to creativity does not address the integral relationship time has with mood. Our moods change over time as we experience day-to-day events and recall that a positive mood is associated with greater creativity and a serious mood with greater problem-solving and analytical thinking. By giving ourselves time to think, we can assimilate our thoughts and learning, and experience a broader spectrum of emotions that enable us to think in different frames of mind and see different perspectives.

Corporations are finally beginning to appreciate the importance of allowing unstructured time to stoke the creative thinking potential of their employees. They are learning that by giving employees time to think, they will encourage more bottom-up innovation.

Google, for example, lets employees take 20 percent of their work time on "pet" projects, because company officials know that people are productive when they are working on things they are passionate about.[116] GE, DuPont and Rubbermaid allow their employees 15 to 20 percent of their work time to pursue whatever projects they like for the same reason.

On a smaller scale, staring out the window, doodling and taking breaks for walks or more vigorous exercise may all appear to be "time off" from work or heaven forbid, play time, in many traditional companies, but those respites can and do improve productivity. The people-as-machines philosophy, where people are expected to focus every minute of their day on work activities, is counter-productive. Progressive

---

115 Sean Silverthorne . July 29, 2002. Interview with Teresa M. Amabile and Leslie A. Perlow. Time Pressure and Creativity: Why Time is Not on Your Side. Harvard Business School

116 Vise, D.A. and Malseed, M. (2005). *The Google Story.* New York: The Bantam Dell Publishing Group, a division of Random House, Inc.

companies are recognizing that increased efficiency results from working in concentrated bursts of activity followed by breaks, similar to Edison's work style.

Best Buy, like so many others, was a company afflicted by stress, burnout and high turnover at its headquarters in Minneapolis. Company officials realized that the old way of doing things had to be changed. So they instituted ROWE, standing for "Results Only Work Environment," also known as the clockless workspace.[117]

Employees can go to the movies in the middle of the day, or go to the gym, or take a nap, or not come in at all, because they are measured not on face-time, but on results. One employee described it as a location-agnostic place with a TiVo way of working – using the metaphor of the digital video recorder that enables the user to find and record television shows, movies, music and videos while fast-forwarding, rewinding and pausing live television. The ROWE program has revolutionized the culture at Best Buy; work is no longer a place where employees go, but something that they do.

Since the program began, average voluntary turnover has fallen drastically while productivity is up an average 35 percent. The Gallup Organization, which audits corporate cultures, says employee engagement at Best Buy, which is indicative of employee satisfaction and a barometer for retention, is way up, too.

Despite these promising findings, however, some managers feel uneasy about relinquishing the control inherent in face-to-face contact and daily 9-to-5 work schedules. Such practices may not be appropriate in every employee situation, because not everyone works in a capacity that allows him to take time for himself during the workday. But in

---

117 Conlin, M. (2006). Smashing The Clock: No schedules. No mandatory meetings. Inside Best Buy's radical reshaping of the workplace. January 2008 from Business Week, Website:<http://www.businessweek.com/ magazine/content/06_50/b4013001.htm>.

situations where it is, hiring the right people for the job and matching the skill sets to fit the job requirements will go along way to priming the intrinsic motivation to get the job done well.

In such workplaces, trust is less of an issue. As our society becomes more educated and work becomes more complex, the work force increasingly includes knowledge workers, who will have a greater need for time to think. The savvy manager recognizes that sitting in a chair is not working. Thinking is.

Chapter 18

The Pursuit of Genius

Talent hits a target no one else can hit; genius hits a target no one else can see."

Arthur Schopenhauer

At 27 years of age, he could neither count to ten nor tell left from right. He needed round-the-clock supervision. Without caregivers, he could not dress or feed himself. He was blind, autistic and severely learning-impaired. Yet after listening to a melody only once, he could play it on a piano without error. In fact, he remembers every piece of music he has ever heard, right down to which piece of music each instrument is playing. Derek Paravicini is one of only 23 autistic savants in the world.

Derek was born prematurely at only 25 weeks, weighing less than three pounds. His parents noticed early on that he had severe disabilities, apparently caused by an overdose of oxygen. They saw that he couldn't distinguish between light and dark. In their desperation to find things that stimulated him, they gave him a plastic, toy organ, when he was around 18 months.

While walking with his parents at the age of four, Derek heard the sound of a little girl playing the piano. He broke free from his parents, headed toward the sound, then pushed the girl out of the way and began playing in her place. While he had had some exposure to a plastic keyboard, it was clear that he had never had a lesson because he struck

Patricia Harmon, Ph.D.

at the keys with his nose, elbows and even his feet. That didn't stop him from playing a wonderful rendition of *"Don't Cry for Me, Argentina."*

Today, Paravicini lives at the Royal National Institute of the Blind College in Surrey, where he spends much of each day at the piano -- except, of course, when he is out playing for his immense international audience.

Groundbreaking innovations are often associated with genius, but it appears that genius has many definitions. Is Derek Paravicini a genius? To answer this question, and to gain insight into genius, we can examine the many definitions and understandings of the word.

The Savant syndrome is a rare condition in which persons have one or more areas of limitations, according to Wikipedia. Savants often have a prodigious memory, says clinical professor Darold Treffert, of the University of Wisconsin Medical School, although that memory is very narrow, and there is little understanding of how the facts fit together.

This might sound impressive, but remembering every detail makes it impossible to form intelligent summaries of details, which, as Treffert says, is the basis of all intelligent thought and communication. The ability to forget is just as important in the brain as the ability to remember. Savants engage in a sort of hyper-focusing, like a car spinning around and around because its steering wheel is stuck in a right turn position.[118] Savants can focus on the details, but not on the whole.

Brain imaging studies are now beginning to support the theory that the condition of savant is caused by damage to the left lobe with the right lobe compensating.[119] Savant syndrome can be congenital, or it can be acquired following brain injury or disease later in infancy, childhood, or

118 Treffert, Darold. A. Savants and us. Website: ttp://geniusblog.davidshenk.com/2007/03/savants_and_us.html March 7, 2007
119 Treffert, Darold A. and Gregory L. Wallace (2003). "Islands of Genius" (PDF). *Scientific American, Inc.* Retrieved on 2009-02-20.

adult life. Certain patients who develop frontotemporal dementia (FTD), who often suffer from an impaired ability to express and understand language, as well as the ability to read and write, can paint beautifully even without any prior talent.[120] These researchers suggest that the astonishing skills of savants, whatever the type of artistic endeavor, are latent in everyone, but not normally accessible without FTD. To prove this, they simulated this type of brain impairment in healthy people by directing low-frequency magnetic pulses into the left fronto-temporal lobe and, indeed, caused improvement in their drawing capabilities.[121]

Another autistic savant, Alonzo Clemons of Boulder, Colorado, can sculpt a perfect wax replica of an animal in less than 20 minutes from a fleeting glance of it on a television screen. It will be correct in proportion, and every detail and fiber. Yet he could not feed himself or tie his shoes. He was a regular child until he suffered brain damage as a result of a fall. Clemons is now recognized as one of the world's most remarkable savants and has been featured on programs such as 60 Minutes, Geraldo, and the Discovery Channel's World of Wonder.

There are mathematical savants, artistic savants and savants with outstanding knowledge in fields such as history, neurophysiology, statistics, navigation, and spatial ability. This is the kind of genius that some describe as raw talent and intelligence, a product of nature. Undoubtedly, it is profound, strange and mysterious. This genius characterizes the Mozarts of the world, who could write five sonatas before noon, but it cannot explain how.

These examples provide a unique window into the brain with regard to defining and measuring intelligence. There is the popular,

---

120 Snyder AW, Mulcahy E, Taylor JL, Mitchell DJ, Sachdev P, Gandevia SC (December 2003). "Savant-like skills exposed in normal people by suppressing the left fronto-temporal lobe". *J. Integr. Neurosci.* 2 (2): 149–58

121 ibid.

albeit controversial, general theory of intelligence that quantifies what is common to the scores of intelligence tests, known as the Intelligence Quotient ("IQ"). A score of 90–109 on the IQ is said to show normal or average intelligence, 110-119 to show superior intelligence and over 140 to show evidence of genius or near genius.

You can become a member of Mensa, an international society known for its intelligent members, if you have an IQ of 130 or above. Mensa says its cutoff restricts membership to the top two per cent of the world's population by this measure; organization officials say there are 100,000 Mensans in 100 countries throughout the world. If a high IQ is a marker of genius, then it calls into question the savant population who would not achieve these measures.

In a 2002 study, Dean K. Simonton showed that the average IQ of 64 eminent scientists was around 150, fully 50 points higher than the average IQ for the general population.[122] And most of the variation in IQs, which is about 80 percent, Simonton says, is explained by genetics. But even he says that IQ isn't the whole story. He says that the rest is intelligence, enthusiasm and endurance.

Historically, there has been a great deal of controversy over what intelligence is and whether it is hereditary or nurtured by the environment. Webster's dictionary says it is one's "capacity for learning, reasoning, understanding, and similar forms of mental activity; aptitude in grasping truths, relationships, facts, meanings, etc."[123] But there are differences in how individuals and groups score that go against egalitarian views.

As Daniel Seligman author of *A Question of Intelligence: The IQ Debate in America* says, according to IQ tests, "the rich have more mental

---

122 Simonton, D.K. (2009). *Genius 101*. New York: Springer Publishing, LLC.
123 Dictionary.com

ability than the poor. Especially troublesome in an age of affirmative action, blacks and Hispanics score significantly lower than whites on average. Whites in turn score a bit lower than Asian Americans, which also counts as bad news in many precincts. Men and women have the same average scores, but men tend to be somewhat overrepresented at the tails of the distribution curve, meaning that more of them are in the high-talent ranges above, say, IQ 140. (Men are also overrepresented among mental defectives, a fact that does not mollify feminist critics of IQ testing.) An irresistible implication of these data (and clearly biased) is that many of the advantages flowing to the most privileged members of American society may have been legitimately "earned."

Howard Gardner, an American psychologist from Harvard University known for his theory of multiple intelligences, agrees that the rare condition of savant syndrome argues against a single generalized intelligence.[124] Instead, he espouses his theory of multiple intelligences, which include:

- Visual/spatial – the ability to perceive the visual. People strong in this form of intelligence tend to think in pictures.

- Verbal/linguistic – the ability to use words and language. These people have highly developed auditory skills.

---

124 Gardiner, H. (1993). *Frames of Mind: The theory of multiple intelligences.* New York: Basic Books

- Logical/mathematical – the ability to use reason, logic and numbers. These people think conceptually in logical and numerical patterns, making connections between pieces of information.

- Bodily/kinesthetic – the ability to control body movements and handle objects skillfully. These people express themselves through movement.

- Musical/rhythmic – the ability to produce and appreciate music. These people are musically inclined and think in sounds, rhythms and patterns.

- Interpersonal – the ability to relate to and understand others.

- Intrapersonal – the ability to self-reflect and be aware of one's inner state of being.

Gardner has been criticized for this theory because he uses the word "intelligences." Critics say he is simply describing what other people call talents or personality types.

Yet another description of genius, this one espoused by Anders Ericsson, Professor of Psychology at Florida State University, is simply the notion of hard work and endurance.[125] This description is characterized by what he calls the 10-year rule, by which, it is said, it takes at least 10

---

125 Ericsson, K.A., Krampe, R.T. and Tesch-Romer, C. (1993). The role of deliberate practice in the acquisition of expert performance. *Psychological Review 100*, v. 3, 363-406.

years (or 10,000 hours – which translates to slightly more than three hours of practice daily for 10 years) of dedicated practice for people to master most complex endeavors. Ericsson points out that Mozart, who was supposedly the greatest child prodigy of all, did not complete his best work until he had spent 20 years composing several hours a day.

Win Wenger, former college teacher in Gaitherburg, Maryland and prolific author in creativity and accelerated learning is another pioneer of intelligence studies who feels that geniuses are people who have stumbled upon a way of perception that widens their channel of conscious attention, bringing into focus their subtle, unconscious awareness. In other words, genius is all about de-conditioning, or bypassing the conscious, which is to be able to look past what we accept as knowledge and see what is too obvious to be noticed.

Where does personality play into all of this? Personality traits also matter, according to Simonton. Geniuses tend to be "open to experience, introverted, hostile, driven, and ambitious."

He also mentions the famous case of the Scottish biologist, Alexander Fleming, who discovered penicillin. Fleming was regarded as a brilliant researcher, but quite a careless lab technician. It was only by chance that he noticed that a culture of Staphylococcus had been contaminated by a mold, which led to this famous discovery. Is that genius? This example seems to be more about serendipity, with chance favoring the prepared mind.

With no agreed-upon definition of what genius is, the possibilities seem to include a brain abnormality that unleashes latent ability, high IQ, multiple intelligences, hard work and endurance, and making the unconscious conscious.

Perhaps the better question is not what genius is, but what it does. If we include the traits that are often used to describe genius as imagination, uniqueness and innovative drive, then we can ask what outcomes are associated with the attainment of genius. There is no shortage of programs offering ways to increase genius because it is tied to success, rewards and fame, some or all of which are commonly thought to enhance one's life.

Perhaps Marie Curie, a physicist and chemist and the first person to have received an unprecedented two Nobel prizes, said it best. She saw the world around her with a childlike sense of wonder. She described a scientist in his laboratory not as a mere technician, but also as a child confronting natural phenomena that impress him as though they were fairy tales. We go back to the intrinsic factors that drive people to do what they do, with an attitude of intense curiosity.

Developing the mind of an innovator is a far more productive and rewarding endeavor than pursuing genius. All too often, genius is regarded as a rare gift, which, in effect, draws the line between those who have it and those who do not. Once a thing is described as a gift, those who do not have it are excused from trying. It is unattainable. The mind of an innovator, on the other hand, is attainable, as you have seen. It is multi-faceted, fertile and stimulating, and its benefits are everlasting.

Chapter 19

Self-Belief Is the Foundation

If I asked you to pretend that I am a psychiatrist and you are my patient, and then asked you to say the first word that comes to mind when I say something, we'd be playing a game of association.

If I said "bread," you'd probably say "butter." If I said "coffee" you'd say "caffeine" or "liquid" or "morning" or something like that. If I asked you to describe a person who is good at math, you'd say "smart." That's because mathematics is, by and large, difficult for many people. We tend to think that when it comes to math ability, you either have it or you don't, as if it is something that is innate. Evidently, it is not.

In his book "Outliers," Malcolm Gladwell, New York writer and social historian, argues convincingly that you can actually predict which students will be good at math by seeing how long they persist in answering questions on a math and science questionnaire.[126] Case in point: every four years an international group of educators administers a math and science test, called the Trends for International Mathematics and Science Study (TIMSS) to students around the world. These students must also fill out a 120-item questionnaire that is tedious and unrelated to math, asking things about their parents' education levels, their home lives and so on. Students often leave as many as 10 or 20 questions blank.

What is remarkable is that Erling Boe, an educational researcher at the University of Pennsylvania, noticed that if you ranked countries by how many of these questions were completed by the students, and then compared that to their international rank on the math portion of the test,

---

126 Gladwell, M. (2008). *Outlier: The story of success.* New York: Little, Brown and Co.

you would find that the two rankings were exactly the same. In other words, those students who persistently plowed through all the non-math questions also did the best job on the math questions. This suggests that persistence is an important emotional ingredient in the achievement of math skills. Aptitude is just as important as attitude.

We have seen that attitude is also important in developing the mindset of an innovator. Perhaps the most pivotal criterion, one that is considered the sine qua non of all achievement and close cousin to persistence, is self-belief. It is a characteristic that waxes and wanes throughout life, and unfortunately, can be the hardest to maintain in the business world, especially when rigid hierarchies are in place.

The Precariousness of Self-Belief

For them, appearances mattered. They were three professionals in a well-known international law firm.

Gloria Anderson was the most senior, and one of the first women to make partner. She had been at the firm for 16 years, and was considered extremely bright and aggressive. She radiated self-confidence. You didn't become partner if you had any self-doubt. And why would she? Coming from a family of means, she had everything she had ever wanted. She went to one of the best Ivy League schools in the country. She alternated summers between the family estate in the Hamptons and Paris, where she learned to speak French fluently. She was of the class that used the term 'summered' as a verb.

Her father, the CEO of an investment bank, mentored her with pride, realizing that his bright daughter would go far. She was the son he never had, but she more than made up for that with her ambition and drive, which he fostered at every opportunity.

Now she had made it: She had pushed her way through the glass ceiling and was at the top of an elite firm where high-ranking government officials had offices and high-profile people made up the client list. It helped that her own family connections brought business to the firm, and she enjoyed the deference shown to her by peers and subordinates.

Her two colleagues, both junior to her, were honored to be working with her. She was demanding and the hours were long, but if you could survive the aggressive pace, you earned your stripes with her. They tolerated her occasional yelling and her biting comments, because she could make or break your chance to become partner.

One of the two, Lawrence, a lawyer in his late 30s, actually enjoyed the rancor at times, priding himself in his ability to argue. He often bragged that he was a recreational debater. His laconic style didn't make him a lot of friends, but he was respected because of his quality work and contributions to the firm. His athletic prowess impressed others and came up in informal discussions. During his college days, he had been second in line for the Davis Cup Tennis Championship, which was quite an achievement. And he never tired of putting on a show of displaying his tennis skills at the firm's yearly retreat.

Brian, the other member of the trio, was in his early 40s. He had not yet made partner. This was true not because he wasn't capable, but rather simply because he didn't get an opportunity to go to university until later in life. Unlike most of his peers at the firm, he had come from a lower-middle-class background. He worked several jobs to pay for law school, and that meant that he had to cut his course load, too, which lengthened the time he took to earn his degree. But that was behind him now. He considered himself fortunate to have gotten into this prestigious firm, especially because he had no connections to important people or any notable athletic skills. Perhaps it was because he had gotten excellent grades, although the other lawyers there had also, he pondered. Maybe he was a token middle-class hire. No matter. He wasn't going to question a good thing.

The three were discussing the tax implications of incorporating a client's subsidiary company. The tax law had been amended recently, and the interpretation of it was ambiguous at best. I was a young administrative assistant at the time sitting in on the meeting to take notes for them. I was a new employee, having joined the firm a few months previously, working full-time while attending university part-time.

Gloria: "I advised NewTech that this initiative has some profound implications for the parent company. Their distribution channels will be affected if they change their transfer pricing practices."

Lawrence: "Well, I've gone through the contracts and there is no obligation for them to maintain their pricing structure past the end of this year."

Brian: "No, there isn't, but it's a contentious area. I have an article here that explains how Jim Nolan over at Smith, Thompson has interpreted this, and it's quite creative. Take a look," he said, handing copies to Gloria and Lawrence. The three scanned the article in silence.

I then said: "If you don't mind my saying so, Mrs. Anderson, there is a multi-national company that has just addressed this issue with their Latin subsidiary and...."

Gloria looked at me with a hint of surprise on her face, clearly not accustomed to interruptions by others, and especially not office staff members.

"Do you have a law degree, Miss, uh, whatever your name is?" she asked, her eye contact piercing and disdain dripping from her words.

Even though I had worked at the firm for only a short time, I had seen Gloria many times in the hallways. Although we had never spoken, I had incorrectly assumed that she would have at least recognized me as someone familiar.

Gloria looked pointedly at Lawrence as I began to respond. Lawrence's expression showed agreement with Gloria's sentiments.

"Well, no, but I am in an M.B.A. program, and we were just learning about a case very similar to…"

Gloria's eyes went from Lawrence straight to Brian before I finished my reply. "Brian, call Ed in tax and pick his brain. I think he has some experience with this. Get back to me by Friday."

"Sure," Brian said, glancing at me and shifting in his chair. Clearly uncomfortable with Gloria's dismissal, he flashed me a quick smile as if to reassure me that me appreciated my comment. I looked down to avoid eye contact with all of them, an attempt to get some respite from the embarrassment of what had just happened, but it didn't work. Lawrence was doodling on his notepad, thinking of which restaurant he might go to for a nice leisurely lunch.

"I think we're done here," Gloria announced, her tone saying clearly that there was to be no more discussion. She strode from the room with the self-importance of a person who has control.

For Gloria and Lawrence, and perhaps less so for Brian, this incident was a minor, unimportant annoyance, quickly forgotten. But for me, being so young and new to the professional world, it left an indelible mark on my psyche.

If this had been an isolated incident, I could have dismissed it as rude behavior by an insensitive boss. But it wasn't. The firm had a distinct pecking order, and it didn't take long to learn where you fit. That incident was the first of many in which I, and many like me, were treated like second-class citizens. It seemed an accepted rule: that was the way things were, and putting up with abuses of power was a rite of passage to more senior roles.

It is an old psychological tenet that the harder you work for something, the more you appreciate its rewards. No doubt that's true. But somehow the Darwinian phrase "survival of the fittest" has become the excuse for demarcating a line between the senior team and others in the company. This phrase is offered as a justification of, and explanation for, the notion that the strongest and most talented individuals make it to the top. The implication is that everyone else is lesser.

This phrase, though, is, in fact a misleading and incomplete explanation of Darwin's theories.

The true meaning of the phrase is that any organism that is capable of reproducing itself on an ongoing basis will survive as a species. That capability belongs not only to the "fittest" ones. Fitness is the average reproductive output of genes in a gene pool, not to be confused with physically fit meaning biggest, fastest or strongest. Physical fitness does not necessarily lead to reproductive success.

By contrast, what happens in strong hierarchical environments like this law firm is that many of the people who ascend the ladder either fight hard to protect their turf because they have struggled so hard to rise, or they end up battle-scarred. Either way, such people don't have much time and energy left to mentor and develop the people below them. Much of the talent around them and beneath them is left untapped.

Even without abuses of power, it takes self-belief to treat others as equals, particularly those above you in the hierarchy. If you believe that the company does not want your input, you will probably keep your thoughts and ideas to yourself and come to feel resentful and unappreciated as I did. Creativity and innovation then become dormant in the organization, and thus talented employees are driven out the door when job markets are strong. When the balance of power lies with the company, for example, when fewer jobs are available, the employee turnover will not be as high, but people will just put in time, doing what they have to do and no more. That spells stagnation. Employee engagement suffers.

According to the U.S. Conference Board, "fewer than one-half of American workers say they are satisfied with their jobs.[127] Although a certain amount of dissatisfaction with a job is to be expected, the extent of dissatisfaction is somewhat unsettling, as satisfaction is part of what keeps employees motivated and productive on the job."[128] Engaged and motivated employees are usually those who feel heard and valued.

Creativity and innovation require risk-taking, regardless of the culture of the company, and it is a virtual certainty that limited innovation will be achieved without risk-taking. What differentiates the risk-taker from the non-risk-taker is self-belief. It takes great courage to go against current trends and break new ground.

A healthy self-belief shows up in traits like flexibility, intuitiveness, independence, comfort with change and, of course, confidence to take risks. When you believe in yourself, you trust your inner signals, intuitions and ideas. You learn from others, but you value your own insights and thoughts. Your mind is less subservient to the thoughts of others, and you can withstand criticism without being struck down by it. That is what gives you the strength to champion an idea through to fruition.

---

127 U.S Job Satisfaction Declines, The Conference Board, Feb. 23, 2007 Website: http://www.conference-board.org/utilities/pressDetail.cfm?press_ID=3075.
128 ibid.

As it turned out, I stayed at the company for another two years while I finished my degree. It was a long time to experience put-downs and dismissals by Gloria and various other senior members of the firm. I did not look for other employment because I had a busy course load, and while that decision was understandable, it was to my detriment. My self-belief had become impoverished.

There is an asymmetry in how we feel emotion, and managers need to be aware of this if they want to get the best out of their employees.

Negative emotions are more enduring than positive ones.[129] Pleasure needs continued reinforcement and pain can persist on its own. In other words, we get used to events that previously delighted and caused us joy, so that we need to continue experiencing more positive events in order to feel pleasure. We do not get used to harassment or humiliation. Think of your last embarrassment in a meeting. It can feel as fresh as if it just happened. Even in its absence we continue to feel its effects. In giving feedback to employees, one negative comment can wipe out four positive ones. Managers can give the same feedback in a motivating or de-motivating way.

Type of Feedback:	Example:
De-Motivating:	"Your sales are down because you're not giving the clients what they want."
Motivating:	"You will increase your sales if by asking the clients these types of questions..."
De-Motivating:	"You don't stand a chance of being promoted unless you apply yourself more."
Motivating:	"All you need to do is add three or four more prospecting calls to your day and that could open up the possibility of a promotion down the road."

129 Frijda, N. (1998). The laws of emotion. *In Jenkins, M., Oatley, K.. Human Emotions: A Reader*. Massachusetts: Blackwell Publishes, Inc. pp. 270-287.

You never know when an insight will hit you, but when it does, it can come with the force of a tidal wave. That is what happened to me one day during a conversation with Brian.

It was a simple comment, one that would not have resonated with me except that I was ready to hear it. They had been working on a project they were about to present to a client. We had just reviewed the presentation summarizing our findings. It was obviously comprehensive, well thought out and sure to impress the client.

Me: "Well, what do you think? Do you think it's good enough?"

Brian: "What do you think, Pat?"

Me "It doesn't matter what I think – what matters is what the client thinks."

Brian: "You've worked on this harder than I have, Pat, and your research has been thorough. But I want you to tell me what you really feel about this. It matters to me, and it will matter to the client."

Me: "Oh, I … I think it's actually quite … uh … yeah, comprehensive." I stumbled on my words because I was not accustomed to being asked about my true feelings about anything. It was startling.

Brian: "Tell me why you believe it. Tell me why I should believe in you, Pat, as if I'm the client." Out of kindness, he pushed me, because he knew that I had self-doubts, and needed to be rid of them. "It is your right to have an opinion, you know."

It was then that it hit me. A simple, almost unnoticeable comment had the effect of a slap across my face. A right to have an opinion. I said it to myself over and over. I had known it intellectually, of course, but I had never really felt it. And now, with Brian's prodding, the wheels were in motion.

With some soul-searching and work on building my self-esteem, it took some time for me to regain my self-confidence and believe in myself. And in less than a year after Brian made his comment, I left the company to start my own consulting firm, feeling more confident than I ever had. Having been a hard-working, loyal employee, it was the company's loss, but my gain. I went into my new venture with an awareness of the work it would it take, and an understanding that it was normal to make mistakes along the way.

Without developing a greater self-confidence, I would not have been able to stop taking criticism and persistently follow my goals. It was then that I learned some creative thinking techniques as part of my self-development, not realizing how valuable they would be. As my creativity emerged, with the new freedom I gained, my self-belief was reinforced. My clients came to rely on me for creative solutions, because my vista had opened up as a result of my self-belief and confidence.

When you are strong in these characteristics, you can afford to focus your sights outwardly, exploring new areas. You have less of an inclination to play it safe with the familiar. For me, it was the beginning of a very fulfilling career. I learned that the barriers I had faced were only my own self-imposed limitations. And as I explored new options and found new talents, my curiosity grew and my attitude toward self-risk developed. When I look back on it now, I realize that I was developing the mindset of an innovator.

Improving one's self-belief has profound consequences in the world of creative thinking because it amplifies the creative effort. Think of self-belief as the amplifying force, creative thinking as the set of directions, and innovation as the outcome. The stronger the force, the greater the ability to jump the inevitable hurdles that stand in the way of innovation.

Chapter 20

Harnessing Innovation in the Corporate World

A global pharmaceutical company that had just undergone a six-month executive development initiative had assigned 60 managers to the task. As part of their development, they had learned, among other things, some creative thinking tools, and they had spent that past few months applying those techniques to projects. Working in teams, they were assigned various tasks requiring fresh thinking and resolution. Today, each team would present its analysis and recommendations to the executive vice president, who listened intently.

When they were done, he sat shaking his head in near-disbelief. "This is an epiphany," he said. "The innovative strategies that have come out of this are far greater than anything I expected. You have demonstrated a deep understanding of the issues we face and have broken new ground in forming the culture of innovation we need. You are all living proof that we have the right talent and ability under one roof."

Then he said something that he never said without first discussing it with the rest of the senior team: "Your recommendations are approved."

Why would this leader be so surprised? The company nominated the attendees for this program, ensuring that only the best and brightest would attend. This same leader had attended other programs in previous years and sat through presentations that he said he found to be mildly interesting.

This year was different for two reasons. It was the first time the executives attending had learned some skilled creative thinking techniques. It was also the first time they had worked together, since two competing firms had just completed a corporate merger.

The cultures at the two companies were very different. In normal circumstances, the cultural differences could have significantly hindered communication between team members. This leader knew all too well that this truly was an experiment to see how well they could fuse their differing philosophies, attitudes and practices, and the test was a success. The actual mechanism to make this happen, though, was not simply the experience of working together. It was the nature of the thinking process itself.

When people in teams engage in structured, creative thinking sessions, they get to hear one another express thoughts that are not part of the normal work day, as they delve deeper into their minds and those of their teammates.

They bring themselves personally to each challenge and each thought-provoking question. No longer are they the products of their job descriptions.

That is true because thinking creatively requires you to scan the vast databank in your mind -- all of your experiences, memories, perceptions and opinions -- to come up with a solution. That brings forth you as a total person, not just the piece of you that gets the job done. Colleagues start to see your depth, talents, enthusiasm and uniqueness that you bring to the job, as they too, begin to more fully recognize their full value.

Even when these sessions have multiple levels of hierarchy, if they are done well so that everyone is treated as an equal, the creative endeavor will give each person a voice. Often, managers see for the first time the true extent of the people on their teams. As ideas catch on, they start to get excited about the prospects.

With such a session, conversations are truly collaborative and the participants designing a collective vision with energy and even passion. This executive, who had lived through a corporate merger years before, recognized afterward that the inevitable conflict and competitiveness that are normally expected from the integration of two management groups did not happen. In its place, through the creative process, this newly formed peer group witnessed the unleashing of the best from each group member.

In the corporate world, creativity and innovation are processes more than products. The work of making innovation a systemic, replicable and enduring process ultimately comes down to the actions of leaders and how they build self-belief in their people. Good leaders know that self-belief unlocks the door to successful innovation. Innovative leaders who help develop creativity in their employees communicate with inspiring words, then follow through on those words with actions.

Such leaders:

Set the Right Tone. Creativity is a function of enthusiasm, motivation, experience and self-belief. Good leaders are confident in their people, and make that known; they let their teams know that they have support all the way. Good leaders make it easier to take initiative and contribute new ideas by breaking down the barriers of bureaucracy and hierarchy that inhibit the flow of information. These leaders find the resources necessary for their people to innovate.

Set Goals for Innovation. Innovation should be a part of everyone's job, but it is not always easily measured. Wherever possible, define the metrics of innovation: number of ideas generated, number of prototypes in trial, percentage of revenue from new products. People do what gets measured, so measure it where you can. Be mindful, however, that people have competing demands on their time, and ensure that managing the measurements does not take the place of increasing innovation.

Encourage Non-Mandated Initiatives. Many creative acts occur unexpectedly, outside the formal lines of a job description. Most people truly want to be creative, and if they are encouraged to follow up on their non-mandated initiatives, they will likely work from a perspective of intrinsic motivation. In the corporate world today, most people are overloaded with work and feel that they cannot complete their assigned tasks. But in this knowledge-based economy, people need time to think and assimilate their thoughts, as well as keep their eyes open for unexpected creative acts.

Recognize risk-takers. Encourage small wins and grassroots innovation. If an employee comes up with a good idea that you implement, recognize and praise that employee publicly. Then take the opportunity to send a message to everyone saying that challenging the status quo is welcome. As Richard Branson says: "Business risk is unaffordable if it will knock him out or be catastrophic to his business. That makes everything else fair game."

Reward failure. Nothing crushes innovation like a fear of failure. If an employee makes an honest attempt to try something new and different and then fails, do not automatically criticize or blame. A bad idea offered in good faith may indicate a need for that employee to learn more about the company or market. Labeling is a bad idea in the first place. It is usually a sign that you are the one with a developmental need to understand how creativity and innovation are fostered, not the employee! Remember, if you use the creative thinking tools in this book, you can always find ways to use what seems to be a bad idea as a stepping-stone to more ideas. One way is to force yourself to see what is positive about that idea, and build upon that, or look beneath the idea and pull out the concepts. Know that if you are going to succeed with innovation you will have many "failures" along the way. Think of them as necessary steps to getting it right. Deal with them positively.

Rewarding Failure

Richard Branson of Virgin Atlantic did this when he promoted a manager who made a decision that cost the company more than £30 million.[130] He had been responsible for installing a new "lie-flat" seat that didn't work. The seat reclined to be flat but not parallel to the floor. Sitting in the seat gave the passenger the feeling of sliding down, and the seat also sank down toward the floor. All this took place when a top Virgin competitor, British Airways, had launched an impressive lie-flat business class seat. Dismissing the employee, Branson said, would have sent the wrong message to other Virgin Atlantic managers, effectively killing its forward-thinking culture.

Assign Role Responsibilities to Emphasize Intrinsic Motivation. There are limits to what you can ask an employee to do, but if you can assign them work that taps into their intrinsic motivation, you won't have to ask them. Work isn't work when you enjoy doing it. The

---

130 SumUp: Richard Branson on innovation and the implications. Retrieved May 15, 2009 from http://www.unitedbit.com/richard-branson-on-innovation-worth-risking-and-supporting, May 10, 2008.

ultimate success in doing this is when you achieve what psychologist Mihaly Csikszentmihalyi Professor of Psychology at Claremont Graduate University, calls flow, that feeling of being in the zone or in the groove. When intrinsically motivated, a person is fully engaged in what she is doing to the point where the task gives her a sense of freedom, and time is ignored. Leaders find out what intrinsically motivates their employees.

Cut Across Boundaries. Support systems can let employees communicate across departmental boundaries to cross-pollinate ideas. Ensure that every employee knows how the company works and where to go to find expertise and resources. Don't stop there: Cut across the company's boundaries and tap into the insights and knowledge of customers, competitors, universities, investors, inventors, suppliers and anyone else you can think of who could be helpful.

Invest in Creative Thinking Training. Creative thinking is an attitude coupled with skills that are learned and practiced. Arming employees with the skills to think creatively will unleash the talent and abilities that otherwise might never be used. We are so much more than our job descriptions: Unlocking creative potential can help employees uncover talents they never knew they had, and tap into their intrinsic motivation. That, in turn, will enhance their job satisfaction and fulfillment. It is a win/win situation.

Chapter 21

Why Do Creativity and Innovation Matter?

Why does creative thinking matter so much for the present and the future? Our world is in the midst of a profound change that is calling for new leadership with new solutions. Issues such as global warming, economic crises, war, terrorism, famine and health care are but a few of the significant challenges we face. As Einstein once said, "we can't solve problems by using the same kind of thinking we used when we created them."[131]

The business world holds an inherent paradox between maintaining control of an organization and giving employees the freedom to work at their true creative potential. The very term "organization" is descriptive. During tough times, particularly, fear and anxiety cause knee-jerk reactions, so that we immediately rein ourselves in by taking even more control. We do what we know best – cut costs, downsize and reorganize for greater efficiencies. These are necessary steps, but no more important than ensuring that employees have the right attitude and skill set to think creatively. Without these attitudes and skills, we are destined to stay within the knowledge base as it is received.

At an individual level, people who think creatively can make opportunities for themselves even when life throws them curve balls. It may not happen right away, but by maintaining a mind open to the most unlikely possibilities, people increase their chances of discovering,

---

131 Retrieved from http://www.Thinkexist.com.

growing and expressing their talents to their full capabilities. Consider the case of Sean.

Sean was a maintenance manager at an insurance company for 28 years. He came to Canada in the 1950s as a poor Irish immigrant with minimal education. But in the school of life, he had learned to fix just about anything. In his free time, he tinkered in his garage, repairing his own car and those of his neighbors. He liked to roll up his sleeves and get right down to it, he'd often say.

His quick Irish wit and sunny personality made him a lot of friends – so many, in fact, that his garage became a place where a constant stream of friends of all ages would drop by whenever they saw him there. As always, he would be singing his favorite Irish songs while he worked.

Sean's life may not have been idyllic by some standards, but he was happy, and that was what mattered. He had a wife, three grown children and plenty to be thankful for. Then one day, life changed.

Sean's boss called him into his office and with genuine sadness, told him that he had to let Sean go. The company was not doing well, and a number of jobs were being eliminated. Unfortunately, his was one. Sean told his boss that there were no hard feelings, although he admitted that he was deeply disappointed. He left the office in a daze, and, for the first time in years, walked without a purpose.

Later, at home, as the weeks passed, Sean tried hard not to dwell on the hurdles he faced. He was the major breadwinner in his family, and had not nearly enough money to retire. He had no formal education and at 59 years of age, his chances of getting another job were slim. So he did what he always did to create enjoyment: he went to the garage, turned on his favorite Irish songs, and began to finish a half-done job of changing some spark plugs.

As he leaned over to grab a tool, he spied a magazine someone had left on a shelf. A phrase caught his eye. It was a quote from Louis Pasteur: "Chance favors the prepared mind."

Reading was not something Sean did much of, but he had time on his hands, so he read further. It was a short article about a young entrepreneur who had been laid off a year before, when she was an administrative assistant in a Fortune 500 company. She had taken her buy-out package and had invested it in an infomercial to sell a hair accessory she had designed for women with long hair. Apparently, she liked to dabble in hair accessories and decided to turn her hobby into a business.

The product itself, as far as Sean could tell, was woefully simple. In fact, it didn't impressive him at all, but it was enough to make her over a million dollars, the article said.

"Sounds like a bit of blarney to me," he thought to himself, and got back to tinkering.

Maybe he would open up a garage repair business, he thought. Or maybe a taxi service, because he liked to drive and loved meeting new people.

"Was that the prepared mind that Pasteur referred to?" Sean wondered. There was something about that phrase that intrigued him, but he couldn't say exactly why.

A week later, some family friends called and offered to take Sean and his wife to a new karaoke club in town. Sean had never heard of such a thing, but at the urging of his wife, they went, and had a wonderful time. Sean sang his heart out at the microphone. Although his voice would not have won awards, his enthusiasm would have, so contagious was his spirit. It was exactly what he needed to re-energize himself to look for gainful employment. But this time, it would be different.

The idea hit him with such a force that it felt as if an electric shock had pierced his body. He would drive a karaoke cab!

He blurted out his idea to his wife and friends. They all laughed. Surely he couldn't be serious, his friend said, adding: "I think you've had one pint too many."

Sean laughed too, in his good-natured way, and even though it sounded ridiculous, he couldn't get his mind off of it. Somehow, he just knew that he had to try it.

The next morning Sean immediately went to work imbued with a purpose that had been missing for a while. He spent the next week retrofitting his car with speakers, an amplifier and a sub woofer, and installed a karaoke machine in the back seat. He then put fliers up in the local supermarket and asked his friends to spread the word. In the meantime, he set about getting taxi license and drove friends around town, attaching the speakers on the roof so everyone could hear them sing as they drove by. It didn't take long before customers called for rides.

Sean found that his business turned out to be every wannabe singer's dream come true, and then some. Customers would sing for a host of reasons. They sang occasionally just for a lark because their friends dared them to. They sang to forget their troubles. They sang for the attention. They sang for emotional release. Whatever the motivation, it became evident that, no matter how they felt as they entered the cab, they always felt better when they left it. It was better than going to a therapist, someone said.

There were times that customers would have Sean go around the block several times just so they could finish the song. Customers booked him for long-distance trips, choosing his service over short haul flights. Groups of employees in several companies in the area began to hire him so they could have sing-a-long meetings that were really teambuilding sessions. The business was a huge success, and Sean loved every moment of it. He could have expanded it by hiring other drivers, but he decided to keep it simple.

Nearly a decade later Sean became ill with cancer. While he was in the hospital, his 12-year old grandson came to visit and asked him if he was afraid to die.

"No, son," he said with the lilt that never left his voice. "I've had a good life. Don't ever forget, son, that life is full of ups and downs. The most important thing is to never be afraid to try new things and believe in yourself, even when others don't."

His grandson replied, "I'm going to be taxi driver just like you, Grandpa."

Sean smiled at the boy. "You can be whatever you want, son," he said. "There's plenty of time for you to decide. This probably won't mean anything to you now, but you must always believe you can do anything you want, and you will do well if you are open to new opportunities. Chance favors a prepared mind, y'know. Don't ever forget that."

Epilogue

Shunryu Suzuki, a Japanese Zen priest, says that "in the beginner's mind there are many possibilities, but in the expert's there are few."[132]

We have covered a lot of ground in this book, and if everything could be distilled into one message, it would be this: You have the capability to expand your mind right now and open up a vista of opportunities never before imagined, once you recognize that the limitations that you have learned can be unlearned. You are then ready to expand your repertoire of creative thinking skills and adopt the mindset of an innovator.

In this book, I have shared with you what it takes to develop an innovator's mindset, beginning with the realization that imagination is pivotal to transcending the limitations you have acquired as you have gained knowledge in life. Great breakthroughs of thinking have occurred as a result of such playfulness in the mind. It is those imaginative leaps that propel us outside the proverbial box.

In Chapters 2 and 3, you read about some of the internal and external limitations that can affect our thinking processes, from the emotions that hijack our thinking, causing us to lapse into an all-or-nothing style, to the use of decoys by others in their attempts to control our decision-making as consumers. Once you are aware of these devices, you become able to manage them.

In Chapter 4, you saw how re-capturing the curiosity you had as a child strengthens your ability to question the fundamental assumptions that underlie your thinking and beliefs. Once you are rid of those, there are far fewer boundaries than you had thought. You see with

---

132 Suzuki, S. (1973). *Zen Mind, Beginner's Mind.* Massachusetts: Shambhala Publications, Inc.

greater clarity that the limitations we have accepted are merely social constructions that can be quickly dismantled, and in this way you can instantly open new territories for thought exploration. And with that enhanced sense of curiosity you will benefit more fully from the lessons before us in nature, in the science of biomimicry.

The thinking techniques in Chapters 6 through 13 offer a mélange of options to help you enrich your thinking and shift your perspective to see the world from different vantage points. With metaphorical thinking, you understand how the power of cross-pollinating thoughts helps to visualize new connections. As a variation of that technique, random connections at times tested your patience in tolerating the illogical.

You saw how wishing for those perfect world scenarios is not just an exercise in fantasy. Asking those "what if" questions can break your linear thinking pattern and direct your attention beyond existing limits to cause you to at least consider possibilities beyond boundaries. Buckminster Fuller is one of many people who have helped to changed the world by asking those "what if" questions. Now we see the emergence of shape-shifting, where cars and buildings are designed to actually change their shapes in response to environmental challenges, and where land can be farmed with smaller plots of land yielding significantly larger amounts of crop yields. Within these examples are ideas that will help us address issues like global warming that face all of us. It wasn't that long ago that these ideas and concepts were the stuff of science fiction.

Looking beneath the surface of the evident, we saw the value in recognizing concepts to increase the number of ideas we have. It is a an accompaniment to experiencing the magic of trompe l'oeil, and understanding the neural mechanisms that cause us to see what we *think* we see, not what we actually see. It is imperative to raise our perceptual consciousness and see from many vantage points, including the literal and figurative. We can then avoid taking for granted things we can creatively change.

That led us to the tool of provocation, the grand master of thinking techniques, where deliberately creating an instability in the mind has led to breakthrough ideas and even the emergence of whole new industries.

In Chapters 12 and 13, we saw the group dynamic limiting an individual's thinking, and learned how to bypass that limitation to get the most of each person's creative thinking. We looked at changing the business paradigm from selling ownership of something to selling the use of it, a concept that will surely gain as we face the growing limits of space amidst an increasing population and material goods.

The search for meaning is inherent in all of us. Making eco-sustainability and social capitalism the guideposts for creative thinking can be not only intrinsically rewarding work, but profitable too. From the entrepreneurial Kamens and Sauls, contributions to the greater good are found in products like the iBot and organizations such as Petfinder, and we are encouraged to see a growing number of global companies that are measuring their carbon footprints.

It is a given that resistance to new ideas is fierce, and we can appreciate what others have experienced to make their innovations successful. Were it not for their persistence, self-confidence and unwavering belief, we might never have known and benefited from their innovations. Judah Folkman was ridiculed by colleagues and snubbed at conferences before he found success for his discovery of angiogenesis, a major discovery used in cancer treatment regimens today. Haney and Abbott nearly went bankrupt before they launched Trivial Pursuit. Ruth Handler's Barbie concept was initially viewed as disgusting by mothers.

That was only the beginning as she later faced multiple manufacturing difficulties.

The makers of Crest toothpaste tested over 500 different fluoride compounds before they came up with one that worked, and they had to wait five years for approval by the ADA They then had to educate consumers

All these innovators had to overcome significant challenges that would have deterred many others. The message is clear: it is a foregone conclusion that resistance will happen, and the innovator must expect it and prepare for it.

A positive sign for the innovative spirit is visible in more progressive companies, where a results-only work environment is embraced. These companies are discarding the old people-as-machines philosophy and replacing it with a "TiVo-like" way of working. We saw how unstructured time allows employees to work to their natural time schedule of concentrated bursts of activity followed by breaks. The results are encouraging: such companies are experiencing increases in productivity and decreases in turnover.

We looked at the many conflicting definitions of "genius," asking if genius is possible or even worth pursuing, and coming to the conclusion that developing the mind of an innovator is a far more productive and rewarding endeavor. Genius, even if it were an agreed-upon phenomenon, seems to belong only to a select few, and seems to be something that cannot be developed anyway. Creativity and innovation are open to all and can be developed.

We also looked at self-belief, the sine qua non of character strengths, that differentiates the risk-taker from the non-risk-taker. Understanding the emotional asymmetry attached to positive and negative feedback can help the creative effort. Armed with this knowledge, managers can help sustain innovation while boosting employee engagement.

In Chapter 19 we saw how thinking creatively in a group can help reduce the conflict and competitiveness that occur with corporate mergers. By enabling team members to see and appreciate one another more fully, new colleagues have an opportunity to see each other's depth, talents, enthusiasm and uniqueness. In making innovation a systemic, replicable and enduring process, we looked at the specific actions leaders can take, ranging from assigning roles to emphasize intrinsic motivation to encouraging non-mandated activities to rewarding failure.

Finally, we examined why creative thinking matters. On the global stage we are facing formidable challenges that require our collective will to resolve. Our future will require great innovations, big and small, that will stem from a bold effort, beginning with creative thinking.

As we struggle through tough times at the organizational level, we revert to what we know best: cost-cutting, downsizing and reorganizing, in an effort to get the most from what we have. But that is not enough, because there must also be a method to unleash the talent of every employee to move forward with new thinking. The latter is often sacrificed for the former, which is a mistake because learning to think creatively has many benefits, not the least of which is a mental emancipation that leads to greater personal and professional fulfillment.

We end with the story of Sean who reminds us that opportunities present themselves when we are in a state of readiness, and the key to creativity and innovation is to have a prepared mind.

I hope I have helped you to expand your repertoire of thinking skills so that your mind is more prepared than it once was. Perhaps most importantly, know that these tools level the playing field for you. There will always be people in life who have more advantages and opportunities than others, whether through birth, money, upbringing or other circumstances. Even before we begin our journey through life, we come into the world with inherent differences that make it easier or harder to achieve success, no matter how it is defined. Arming yourself with the innovator's mindset removes many of those obstacles as you flex your mental muscles to transcend them.

Your mind is a vast reservoir, and the techniques in this book are a path to help you dive in as deeply as you wish to go. Immerse yourself. As the philosopher Law-Tzu said in the sixth century B.C., "The master travels all day without ever leaving home." Visit often with the belief that an open mind is an open view. That is the mindset of an innovator.

Appendix

Persist in the Face of Doubt

Developing an innovator's mindset has profound consequences
in all aspects of your life. By opening up your mind, you are opening
yourself to greater opportunities. It is too important to leave in the
hands of others by waiting for validation and encouragement. Think of
how differently our world would have been if these individuals had not
persisted:

- The comments written about the screen test from the testing director
  at MGM were "can't act, can't sing, slightly bald, can dance a little."
  The entertainer was Fred Astaire; he danced for 76 years thereafter.

- This boy "didn't have enough sense," the boss said. He worked in a
  dry goods store and was not allowed to wait on customers because of
  this weakness. That was Franklyn Winfield Woolworth, the founder
  of Woolworths; his store lasted for 23 years, and is now known as
  Footlocker.

- He was fired from two jobs for being "non-productive" and described
  by his teachers as "too stupid to learn anything." He was Thomas
  Edison.

- This "sub-normal" child did not speak until he was four years old and
  did not read until he was seven. A teacher described him as "mentally
  slow, unsociable and adrift forever in foolish dreams." Albert Einstein
  became one of the world's greatest physicists.

- Lacking imagination and having no good ideas, this guy was fired by his newspaper editor. He went bankrupt numerous times, but finally built the largest entertainment company in the world. He was Walt Disney.

- Two popular record companies turned down a recording contract with this group because they believed that guitars were on their way out. The Beatles changed the face of music.

- He was never able to improve his awkward technique playing the violin, but he did enjoy playing his own compositions. That didn't matter much to his teacher, who called him "hopeless as a composer." Beethoven wrote five of his greatest symphonies while he was completely deaf.

And finally, this person had a series of failures:

Age 21: Failed in business

Age 22: Defeated in a legislative race

Age 24: Failed again in business

Age 26: Overcame the death of his sweetheart

Age 27: Had a nervous breakdown

Age 34: Lost a congressional race

Age 45: Lost a senatorial race

Age 47: Failed in an effort to become vice-president

Age 49: Lost another senatorial race

Age 52: Elected the President of the United States

He was Abraham Lincoln.

Breinigsville, PA USA
09 December 2010
250946BV00002B/6/P